the inspired teacher

Skyhorse Publishing books may be purchased in bulk at special discounts for sales promotion, corporate gifts, fund-raising, or educational purposes. Special editions can also be created to specifications. For details, contact the Special Sales Department, Skyhorse Publishing, 307 West 36th Street, 11th Floor, New York, NY 10018 or info@skyhorsepublishing.com.

Skyhorse® and Skyhorse Publishing® are registered trademarks of Skyhorse Publishing, Inc.®, a Delaware corporation.

www.skyhorsepublishing.com

10 9 8 7 6 5 4 3 2

Library of Congress Cataloging-in-Publication Data is available on file.

Cover design by Brian Peterson

Print ISBN: 978-1-63220-341-0
Ebook ISBN: 978-1-63220-838-5

Printed in China

the inspired teacher
Zen Advice for the Happy Teacher

DONNA QUESADA

Skyhorse Publishing

CONTENTS

Preface ix

Preface

Though I have changed the names to protect the identity of my students, the stories in this book are true and are woven into a collection of chapters that may be read chronologically or randomly. These anecdotes are set in the context of a community college, but teachers of every level will identify with the conundrums recounted therein, which are universal to all classrooms.

Most of the events in this book took place during the course of a particularly trying semester, from the familiar first-day ride to campus right through to the end of the course, with its inevitable barrage of emailed grade complaints. I was in a lecture hall with 125 students, where the discord I felt with this group was both worsened by and pivotal in magnifying my already growing feelings of burnout.

Turning to my longtime spiritual practice, I survived that semester and gradually rediscovered the joy that had been progressively declining. It is my wish to take you along with me on what I'll call a spiritual journey and to share with you some of the insights I have learned through my formal training in Zen Buddhism, as well as through my longtime practices—both as a teacher and a disciple—of classical Yoga.

Each chapter concludes with an essential dharma teaching, relevant to the quandary presented. Dharma, in its most basic sense, is the word for Buddha's teachings, and although I am presenting what I hope will be viable lessons for you in these sections, *The Inspired Teacher* is not a how-to book for teachers; rather, it is an intimate portrayal of the often-paradoxical Zen wisdom pertinent to the anecdote. It explores, in the context of unique sketches, my frustrations as a teacher and the lessons I took away from various situations. They are the lessons that would bring me back and that would reveal, time and again, that no matter the situation, it's always about getting your head in the right place first. Resolution starts in our own minds.

The Zen wisdom that concludes each chapter contains the fruits of Buddha's insight, as an enlightened being. He wasn't a god. He was someone who found a way out of his own suffering and dedicated the rest of his life to helping others escape theirs. Pain, loss, and everyday grievances are inevitable, but he showed us how to unshackle ourselves from the additional suffering we habitually bring upon ourselves in the form of mental anguish. To escape this suffering is to wake up. It is to wake up to our own inherent wisdom and to an abiding sense of serenity and equanimity. It is to wake up to that inner light within that rouses our feeling of connection and enthusiasm in all that we do.

Some days, some semesters, and perhaps even some years will be more challenging and more wearisome than others. But my wish is that you find within this series of classroom vignettes a lasting source of encouragement and inspiration. Although I draw from Eastern teachings, the wisdom is for all of us, regardless of personal background, creed, or faith, for inspiration is universal.

Finally, just as a teacher masters her subject by teaching it, a writer writes what she most needs to learn. Thus, when I address you, I am also addressing myself. I write for the both of us. May we find then, together, solace in these lessons whenever we need them. And may we all be inspired so that we may light the way for others.

PART One

·

THE
BURNED-OUT
PROFESSOR

·

1

Driving There
I Think, Therefore
I'm Not

I t was the first day of the fall semester. Escaping from my car radio speakers was the latest news on the Dow Jones slide. It resonated with the direction of my enthusiasm, which was plummeting just as fast. I had just turned in grades last week for the intense six-week summer class that is squeezed in between the two main semesters. That morning, I considered how strange and unnatural it felt to be starting again from the beginning, after having just given the final lecture to the class that finished only a few days earlier. I had invested myself in bringing the students strategically, step by step, through all the new ideas, right through to the end of the course, and to the grand finale of the final exam, only to press REWIND and start again.

Wallowing in my thoughts about how curious it seemed to be starting anew, I stopped at the local coffeehouse, hoping my usual might lift my waning spirits. Then I continued on to campus, where I would trek the familiar route to the lecture hall and greet the new, and bigger, group, because fall brings a new onslaught of students. I would introduce myself, the topics, and set the tone for the sixteen-week semester ahead, hoping to display the enthusiasm they expected and that I expect of myself. It was the first day of school for them, and for many, the first day of college. It would be our first day together, and I was about to set the first impression they would have of me.

The more I indulged my imagination, the more Herculean the task seemed—especially if I allowed myself to get swept up in the scene unfolding in my mind: how I would walk into the classroom, rolling backpack in tow, all eyes on me, their owners wondering what to expect. *That's her.* They would guess it by the rolling bag, and my parking it in front of the big desk in front of the huge room would settle the question. *She looks nice.* Or, *she looks mean.*

I would relieve the bag of its contents—the newly printed three-page roster of unknown names, the stack of double-sided syllabi, and sundry early handouts, while self-consciously avoiding eye contact, defensively recoiling from the weight of their gaze.

While waiting for the green arrow at the familiar Ocean Park light, I entertained myself with vague memories of back-to-school days when I was a kid. Every September, as if in conspiracy with the school calendar, LA's notorious marine layer, whose coolness and softness I now love, would cover the city until noon. Through my young eyes, it was as if the sky was casting a dismal pall over what was supposed to be an exciting reunion of teachers, students, and friends. It was the day that interrupted the lazy and agreeable inertia of summer, the day of the well-known, very palpable, but wholly unspeakable pressure that exists between kids—to size each other up and sort themselves into hierarchical status groups.

At that age, students think the teachers can't wait to get there. It seemed impossible to imagine that teachers had any existence beyond the walls of the classroom. In some unarticulated way, I fancied they must live in the classroom, behind the walls, and then crawl out from some secret hole, every September, eager to get their hands on our thick stacks of papers. I would have been shocked to hear the truth: Teachers sometimes can't wait for you to leave the room, and they want the 3:00 bell to ring more than you do.

Now, as a teacher myself, I've been entrusted with the task of explaining philosophy to curious young minds. Part of my task, in a traditional class on Western philosophy, is to tell them it's based in wonder. From the Greek words for "love" and "wisdom," it is the meta-discipline that seeks an understanding of knowledge—what it is, if it's possible, and if so, what are its limits? In the characteristic spirit of curiosity that laid the template of modern-day scientific inquiry, it eschews dogma in favor of reason and pursues only consistent beliefs that lead to truth.

But I found that truth only happens in the crux of the moment, when the theories and logical wordplay are superseded by the immediacy of the present moment. This state of presence reveals a stillness that was previously concealed.

When Socrates spoke of liberation, he described a freedom that comes from knowing your own mind, from analyzing its sum of beliefs and weeding out the unsupported ones in deference to the verified and true. *The unexamined life is not worth living*, he famously announced. But in the Eastern wisdom traditions, "liberation" means to break free of the hindrance of the mind and its neurotic tendency to examine and overanalyze everything. It is to open up into the vibrancy of the present moment without conditions. It is permission to release all those busy thoughts. It is a gleeful and spontaneous opening that pacifies instantly, what is known in Buddhism, as the *monkey mind.* It is to wake up, and it is to know that this kind of freedom isn't found in theories.

For a teacher fighting the onslaught of burnout, driving to the classroom is worse than being there. It is where you anticipate your day and where you torment yourself, asking incredulously, "Do I really have to talk about *free will* again?" It is exactly where aversion presents itself and where you begin to feel like a broken record, singing the same old verses one more time.

Dharma: The Lesson for Teachers

Thoughts of what the day will bring are future thoughts. The mental checklist of the day's chores are future thoughts. Even the thought of not wanting to teach is a future thought. Catch yourself when you start to sink into them. Don't suppress them; simply observe them. A subtle shift occurs with the mere act of watching. That internal begrudging dissipates. Those thoughts aren't reality; they're ideas, and ideas are future thoughts. Staying out of the *idea* of not wanting to go, and out of the mind that complains, allows you the freedom to enjoy again, whatever the day brings, in real time.

When Zen practitioners say that meditation is hard, it seems incredible that sitting still could be that difficult, but it is because being HERE is not someplace we're used to being. It requires constant reminding to come back. The job of meditating is to do just that. It is the training ground for the mind, where it learns to sit still and stay. Experiment with simply noticing how often you fall into these indulgent *longing and loathing* thoughts. The mind is a time machine, scurrying back and forth between thoughts of the past and of the future, every waking moment of every day. The practice of meditation is supposed to train you for life off the cushion. But even if you don't have a committed meditation practice, the tricks I've grown to love and use are still effective, whether on the cushion or in stolen moments between classes.

When I have my students meditate for just a few minutes in class, some report that it makes them think even more than usual, that it's crazier and busier in their heads than ever before. *No,* I tell them. *It's like that all the time; you just never stopped to notice it before!*

Leave no traces, Zen says.

I was close to their age when I first learned to meditate. With a budding interest in Eastern philosophy, I took it as a college course with a Japanese professor, who told us to call him by his first name, Eiichi. Such a class was an unusual find in the university setting, but the nine of us in the class enthusiastically purchased our *zafus,* or Japanese meditation cushions, lined them up along the wall, and eventually got to the point where we were sitting on them for forty-five minutes per day. Sometimes, after sitting, he would play old subtitled black-and-white video clips of Zen masters talking about things that seemed mysterious to me then. They said to *leave no traces* when we act. I later saw that this message, far from being mysterious, was a reminder to come back to the ordinary, which is right here, right now.

I remember a classmate asking, "What's so great about now?" The professor's simple reply: "Stillness is in the present."

The now-retired professor spoke of the millions of thoughts that obfuscate our minds at any given moment, thoughts that spring back and forth like pogo sticks, from past to future, and back to the past again, never stopping *here*. The catch is that you can't *will* them to stop here because suppression doesn't work. You have to let them settle themselves, and to this end, he gave us the metaphor of the revolving door, the same one I now pass on to my own students. Continuing the process of observation, watch as your thoughts enter the already-crowded lobby of your mind—but watch, also, as they leave again on their own, as if through a revolving door, so long as you don't attach to them.

To attach is to simultaneously resist. It is to willfully bind yourself to the unreal world of thoughts rather than to swim with gusto in the current of life in real time. Those thoughts are the same ones that keep you trapped in the idea that things are going to be tedious.

I am back in my car, and *right now* I'm just driving, and the clouds are beautiful.

Create the liberating habit of proclaiming your presence and the joy that comes with it. Proclaim it with a mantra: *At this moment, I am happy.* It is the only place happiness exists, after all. I find myself unable to contain a smile when I utter it, sometimes several times in a day, in spontaneous bliss, at any given moment. And every time I utter it, I come back.

When I consciously remember to practice presence in this way, en route to campus, I always end up truly enjoying class. I'm fresher and more spontaneous. Anticipating the day in the car is like working twice. The Zen masters would say it is as silly as wearing two heads. You're starting the day before it actually starts.

Coming back is something that gets easier to sustain with practice. At that very instant, resistance magically disappears. It is instantly replaced with inner gladness, the way the slightest crack of the curtain floods the entire room with the morning sun and displaces the darkness in a flash. With true presence of mind, enter your class in a spirit of openness, with a smile and a spring in your step rather than in a clenched-up ball of seriousness.

I shared my mantra with a student once. She confessed the difficulty she had been having with the simple task of staying present. That is precisely what makes it a practice, I told her. The contentment it engenders is a moment-by-moment play, an exercise, a constant coming back, because, like Eiichi said, this is where stillness is. And like the "gap" between thoughts, in meditation, a timeless moment of emptiness is found. Between the disjointed movie scenes and endless montages in your mind, between flashbacks and instant replays of events that happened yesterday, and errands to be run tomorrow, a softness is found: *Aha!* Just a glimmer, a sparkle, and the droplet becomes the ocean. Then, just like that, with a blink, it's gone. But with practice, the glimmer becomes a way of life. You hold it longer. You learn to reside there. You bring the magic of the cushion off the cushion and into the real world.

More than a decade had passed since the days spent staring at the back wall of Eiichi's classroom. I found myself in the sparsely decorated third-floor zendo of an old three-story Victorian house that had been converted into a Zen temple, located in the middle of Los Angeles. The Zen master was giving his weekly dharma talk. I soon called him *Roshi*—the traditional way to address your teacher in Japanese—and he called me *Kaishu*, the dharma name he gave me when I took my Zen precepts.

When Roshi mentioned "spontaneity," I finally understood, in a flash, what I had been explaining to my own students for years. On that day, the soil was fertile and receptive to what it had been impervious to before. My begrudging ruminations in the car were nothing but repetitive skips on an old record, a verse stuck on a loop. Being stuck is being blind to life's endless possibilities, like a sleepy traveler, missing the treasures and the side roads simply because he was stuck and couldn't see.

We never give the same lecture twice. We are not the same teachers we were last year, or even yesterday. Our understanding deepens, and our perspectives change. The students are different, and their questions change. There are ten thousand different ways to broach a topic. Entering into this realization is to experience the spontaneity that comes with it. It is to be present for the interactions with the students in front of you, to laugh with them, to answer them, and to take joy from their curious faces. It is the first time for all of us, a new beginning.

Settling the waves of the ruminating mind—a true liberation.

"*Do not try to stop your thinking. Let it stop by itself. If something comes into your mind, let it come in, and let it go out. I twill not stay long. When you try to stop your thinking, it means you are bothered by it. Do not be bothered by anything.*"

—Suzuki, *Zen Mind Beginner's Mind*

2

Burnout or Boreout
Yes, and Thank You

One mid-morning during the fall, our chairperson passed me in the copy room and asked if I wanted to teach an extra course the following semester. This was a boon, considering the plight of many of my colleagues who had been losing classes since the beginning of the recession.

At the coffeehouse on the way to campus that morning, I had been indulging in fantasies about quitting my job. Totally clichéd ones that involved selling funny snack foods on the beach, like churros, or maybe pineapple spears. I watched the steam rise from the cup I held between my cold hands, savoring every last sweetened sip and escaping further from reality with each comforting swallow. I wondered how I would find the will to talk about whatever it was I had to talk about that day one more time, to take a three-page roll call one more time, to harness the wandering attention of 125 post–high-school kids one more time.

In the copy room, our department chair stacked her papers on the bulk tray, punched in her secret code, and set the old machine in motion, click-clacking and bellowing, spitting papers randomly into side compartments. She was shuffling and sorting, and I knew she was waiting for an answer. The moment felt long, and I thought she might think my hesitation strange, especially coming from one whose enthusiasm had always equaled her own.

I remembered reading about burnout. I remembered the signs and the traps. *Wanting to accommodate.* A classic symptom. *Don't be the yes girl,* my peppy eighty-five-year-old neighbor once reminded me. But I wanted to say yes; I was the one she could count on—the one who jumps to task and finishes it first. I liked her and wanted to please her. *Wanting to please . . .* there it is again.

At the time, I wasn't sure if I was tired of teaching or tired of what I was teaching. And I wasn't even sure what it meant to be tired. Did I just need a break, or was I tired in the way that people are when they're truly disgusted? I was certainly tired of arguing, and that's what my primary subject was all about.

Philosophy, as it is taught in the West, is an argumentative discipline. When I was a grad student, my professors rallied us to *do* philosophy rather than just write about it. I learned quickly what that meant: Argue your points and justify your claims. It was exhilarating to dissect arguments, to pick apart the famous works on the existence of God and free will, and other divided topics, and say which ones work, and which ones fail, and why. But I couldn't ignore my intuitive feeling that the deeper truths would never be wrenched out of the whys and the wherefores, and that all the arguments and logic and deductions would ultimately fall short.

It started to feel like a game—a board game, where you move your marker around a make-believe course and try to advance to the end first. You identify the logical fallacies—the begging questions, the slippery slopes, the false dilemmas, the flimsy straw men, and the never-ending pile of ridiculous appeals. You call out all the unsupported assumptions, and you win. You bask in the self-satisfaction that comes from weeding through the mess of fictitious claims. But the pleasure runs thin quickly, and truth still seems far away.

Following my feelings, I put my attention into my Asian philosophy course, where I could lead students through the enlightenment traditions of the East, leaving behind the arguments of the Western approach. Together we could explore the lives of the mystics and the yogis, and the timeless insights that surpass those dialectic methods. We could explore the domain of higher wisdom—the wisdom that lies somewhere beyond the words and the theories.

But after a while, even my beloved Asian philosophy grew tedious, and my apathy settled in. I deleted interdepartmental e-mails, ignored discussions of dire part-time issues—budget cuts, setbacks, and numerous problems affecting my own future and all of education. It just didn't interest me. I was bored. I showed up for class and then went home.

I smiled a knowing smile when I later saw the movie *Crazy Heart*. I could relate to Jeff Bridges's character. Just as my students would rush up to me after class, proud and anxious to share their opinions on this theory or the other (when all I wanted to do was get to my car), his young backup musicians were just as spirited: "What time should we practice, Mr. Blake?" "When are you comin', Mr. Blake?" Burned out, and reduced to playing in bowling alleys where he couldn't even get a bar tab, he had no intention of showing up any earlier than he had to: "You guys go ahead and practice without me," he'd grumble.

The aging musician was defeated by his own apathy and by a notoriously fickle music industry that sweeps aside the old guys faster than bugs in a restaurant kitchen. Although our stories were different, apathy and weariness are thieves that steal our sense of vitality, without a second's thought about who we are or what our stories are. Bad Blake got a second spin in the end, but it wasn't without the trials that are so often the very source of rebirth and renewed joy.

Dharma: The Lesson for Teachers

Not long ago, I attended a weeklong yoga seminar in San Francisco. I enjoyed walking through Chinatown each afternoon on the way back to my hotel. On a crisp Sunday, I passed a bearded old man with wistful blue eyes, playing clarinet on a busy street corner. The clarinet has always been my favorite instrument, and I told him so. He played my request and then we chatted about Benny Goodman and all the other old greats of a time gone by. In parting, he told me, with tears in his eyes, that although he could have played in a symphony, it meant much more to him to play for the people. I'll never know if that was true, but whether it was or not is not the point.

The point is, our minds contain the wellspring of all distinctions—even the boredom standing opposite everything else that appears (in our imaginations) to be more desirable and more exciting. There is nothing intrinsically boring in this world; after all, *someone* is interested in whatever it is that bores you. My wise friend with the clarinet was grateful just to play. No matter what your circumstances are, there will always be a higher or more attractive position to covet and someone who does it better, whatever it is. So, why not be fine with where you are?

There may be nothing intrinsically boring, but there *are* bored minds. *If you're bored, it's because you're boring,* my Zen teacher said once. I had tinkered with plenty of logical syllogisms as a philosophy student, but this one hit me with a thwack. And it didn't require any truth tables or diagrams. With nothing but honesty as a tool, the conclusion was self-evident: We are the authors of our own weariness and apathy.

The boredom starts with the thoughts that resound through our minds as if on replay. The broken record spins on, pumping out the same refrain, over and over, wearing out the tired old grooves, day after day, serving only to reaffirm the tired old stories we tell ourselves. Yet thoughts are mere cobwebs that turn to dust, never measuring up to the immediacy of direct awareness.

In seeming contradiction, as if someone suddenly bumped the needle on the old player, those thoughts then change. Thoughts are forever capricious in every facet of life. And a thousand subtle, untraceable events contribute to never-ending shifts: You realize you had judged wrongly on first impression, your tears suddenly turn to laughter with a word, your fear turns to relief with a phone call—all kinds of crazy imaginings disappear as seamlessly as the painted orange sky fades into twilight.

Thoughts are as ephemeral as shooting stars. You don't have to believe them. What if you could watch them as if they were amusing scenes in a play? Whether it's a passing impulse, or a relentless preoccupation, they're all thoughts. Whether it's a fly-by-night fancy or a recurrent desire to leave your job when you feel burned out, they're also just thoughts. One is urged on by lust, the other by distress. Both are rooted in desire, and both are thoughts. But you are not your thoughts. A Zen master once compared thoughts to body secretions, vanishing as soon as they appear. And an Indian mystic likened them to graveyards, calling them the repository of all dead things, all the experiences, memories, and fragments of the past that are now like ghosts.[1]

I don't mean to imply that you should never make a change or that you must accept everything with unflinching submission. But by simply becoming aware of the fleeting nature of thoughts, you'll know if and when the time has truly come for change, and you'll know what must be done. You'll know it the way you know when you're in love, or the way you know when you feel sick. It'll be as obvious as when you have something stuck in your eye. We have always been told to *think it through*. But, paradoxically, Zen tells us that this is exactly what gets us into so much trouble. To be sure, we've never been more rational as a species, but at the same time, we've never been more confused and depressed.

Reality must be embraced as it is—its eternal moment welcomed without all the second-guessing and second thoughts that keep us feeling cut off and stuck in our heads. Our most crucial moments reveal that it is the tangled mess in our heads that always gets in the way. When the actor gets lost in his own thoughts, he forgets his lines; when the relay runner replays last night's conversation in her head, she misses the starting gun. We've all missed our freeway turnoff because we were lost in some big

1. Osho, *Intuition: Knowing Beyond Logic*. New York: St. Martin's Griffin, 2001.

fantasy, and in the classic example of the samurai warrior, when he hesitates for even a moment to think it through, he gets a sword right through his chest.

You don't think your way back to joy; you open to it. It's not to say we should walk around in a quasi-comatose state—quite the opposite! It is to see what is really here. It is to awaken. And it's not to say that *thinking*, or conceiving of imaginary scenarios in our heads, doesn't ever serve its purpose. You may think through a play in chess, but happiness can only exist in a peaceful, unruffled mind. Living in a state of absolute presence allows you to experience things directly rather than through the filter of a million muddled worries, regrets, fantasies, and judgments. It's not about thinking positively; that just keeps you stuck in your head. It's not about suppressing your thoughts; that just gives them more juice. It's about entering into the intimacy of whatever this moment brings, without agenda-driven conditions, and without the story line we keep coming back to out of habit.

> *When the water is clear, you see the infinite possibilities,* Zen says.

As a murky pond obscures the brilliance of the blushing koi below, when your head is full of your own complaints, it dulls your inner sparkle and makes it impossible to illuminate others. How can you offer anything of value to anyone else if you're lost in your own muddled head? That is really why we teach, after all—to guide others. And that's what makes it a noble profession.

How do you get clear? Turn your attention wholeheartedly to your students. They'll come alive, and you'll no longer have to goad yourself on. You'll enjoy the interplay again. You'll be part of it. There is a magical shift that occurs with this simple shift of attention. The effects you will have on your students are infinite and currently unknown; you will possibly shape the way they proceed in their careers, the way they will vote, the way they will behave as partners and spouses, the way they will raise their kids. When you're open, you open minds, and when you're clear, you clear their doubts as well as your own.

Becoming clear is the purpose of *zazen*, which is seated meditation in Zen. It allows you to experience a deeper stillness, which gives birth to insights that don't dwell in discourse. It allows you to welcome the opportunity to rest your busy mind that is constantly churning and chomping and chewing ideas.

I hope you will try sitting on your own for a few minutes each day. A nice way to start is to simply sit in a quiet spot and mind your breath. Allow it to settle and become slower on its own, and just return to presence each time you find yourself wandering away in reverie or worry. The beauty emerges when you find that gentle balance between alertness and ease.

Even without a committed practice, however, you can still take the first step toward *the backward step*, which in Zen recalls this state of clarity in which you simply become aware of your thoughts without getting involved in them. Like junk mail, they will keep coming, but you don't have to get seduced by their propaganda. Just allow those thoughts to pass through, neither welcoming them nor resenting them. That's what it means to be clear.

The question of whether you're bored with teaching, or with the subject you teach, may just sink to the bottom of the pond with all the other muck. Both are born of the clouded mind—what my Zen teacher calls *the picking-and-choosing mind*. It is the immature mind that wants to be entertained and gets upset when things stop being entertaining, like a kid who gets bored with his toys. There will always be fancier toys in the toy store and a hundred reasons to be bored with what we have.

To all of these excuses, the Zen master would respond by saying you're stuck in a box. Sure, there may be select cases of tedious, repetitive jobs that can be said to contribute to genuine despondency, but those cases are exceptional and outside the scope of teaching. In the work that we do, for the hundred boring things, there are a hundred more interesting things to discover, if you're awake to see them. And if you're truly awake, doting on passing feelings of boredom may start to feel like nothing but an indulgence.

Our perceptions shape the way we experience reality. Whether we live in an enlightened state or a deluded one derives from our state of mind. There is an oft-used metaphor in Zen of a hundred-foot pole. It asks how you might manage to go any further if you're already at the top. It is only the strings of our attachments that hold us back, but like gum stuck to our shoe, every time we try to cut the stretchy strands, they just stick to the scissors. Desires are difficult to sever. *I don't feel like teaching that today; I'd rather teach this. I don't like that student; I prefer this one. I don't like this classroom; I'd prefer that one.* All of this debris that clouds our minds and robs us of the amazing clarity we seek is born of desires.

You are the universe unfolding, Zen says.

Think back to when you first started teaching. You were bubbling with fun and zany ways to get students interested. And then, at some point, you found yourself repeating the same old formulas. Until your mind is clear, you'll do the same thing in any other job you might take. It's like trying to cover up any source of discontent by drinking, eating, gambling, or even traveling; they are all just temporary escapes. Ways of running away. It's not that you shouldn't ever do those things—traveling is fun, as is eating. A good blended margarita can be lots of fun. But wherever you go, there you are, along with your head—that big globe of grievances and grumbling. So being antsy becomes just another unrelenting habit, and the little pleasures in life quickly become crutches. The pattern will repeat itself until that head is clear.

All formulas get old because the current of life is in constant flow. You are different and your students are different, not only from year to year, but from week to week, even day to day; you're just too busy to notice. Creativity blooms when you unfold *with* that flow. You are a part of the unfolding universe; you are the universe itself. There is no separation. Just as there are a hundred ways to get bored, there are also a hundred ways to get interested. And there are countless ways to broach a subject, which will change with the varying context.

The philosophy of emptiness in Buddhism sounds esoteric and is often misunderstood; it is just a word used to express the inexpressible—the absence of separation between this ball of thoughts I call myself and the flow of the universe and the abiding transience of it all. One of the amazing things about art is that it brings forth these inexpressible truths. When Joshua Bell picks up his violin and takes the stage, he isn't thinking anymore of the theory and the training methods. He simply unfolds the melody, and the music comes to life. He is an empty vessel, disappearing into the music. The training already took place, so he has no need to contemplate it anymore. He becomes his violin. When you jump into your classroom, and lose yourself in it, you too are expressing this beauty.

When you lose yourself and jump in, you simultaneously break out of that box. What does the situation in front of you require? A mother knows which child needs more coddling and goes forth without hesitation or puzzling over it to provide that comfort at just the right moment. She is *clear*. This lesson is true in everything we do, at home and at work. Conversations seem boring because of that claustrophobic box in which we continue to reinforce our own preferences, and repulsions. *I don't like race cars; why is this guy talking to me about race cars?* Open up to discover the hundred interesting things about race cars—the aerodynamic shape, the takeoff speed, the handling. How much there is to learn, if we simply pay attention!

Not one thought is worth a second thought,
Zen says.

Next time the internal chatter and resistance start up in your classroom, try a radical experiment. Say, *I don't have to talk about anything today—I'll just ask for questions and see how it goes*. It always turns out to be a great class! The questions lead to great discussions that are usually more relevant and rewarding than that stale old lecture anyway. It's not to say that calculations and projections don't have their place—but that's just it: *They have their place.* Too often those functions slip into nothing but obsessive ruminating that only serves to keep us trapped in our own negative-habit patterns. Pulling out of them doesn't have to be complicated. Have faith in yourself and all the experience you've amassed through your years as a teacher so that you can stop thinking about it, and be *there* to actually experience teaching.

When I was learning languages as a young college student, I found that as long as I continued to translate while listening, I couldn't keep up with the conversation. The reason echoes the same point. While I was busy translating, I was separated from the pure act of listening, lagging behind at a distance—always a step away and a sentence behind, and I would miss the entire conversation. I learned through experience to stop thumbing through my mental translator, because going back and forth kept me stuck in my head. But streaming with the conversation, as it unfolded, freed me up to take in the foreign words as they were, and to respond appropriately, without the extra step of translating. There is a gracefulness about flowing with the current of the exchange in real time.

Yes, and thank you.
—ChiSing

Grace is an unseen but unmistakable quality that shines forth when we work in a state of presence—when we work with ease, without puzzling over it, and moreover, when we work with a total lack of ambiguity.

Although ambiguity is typically defined as uncertainty, its Latin roots give it away. It has more to do with being of two minds, as in the word *ambidextrous*, which describes someone who is equally adept with both hands. Grace comes from the clarity of *not* being of two minds, from throwing ourselves wholeheartedly into the task at hand with no ambiguity or doubt.

Grace is most beautifully expressed when we simply do, without being overwhelmed, and when we act, with no thought of personal reward—when we accept the circumstances, saying only *Yes, and thank you* to reality as it is. Say it out loud. Repeat it as a mantra: *Yes, and thank you.*

PART TWO

·

THE
CLASSROOM

·

3

Add Codes
The Door Is Open

One of the certainties of the first day of class is the need to address the multiple, inevitable, and often-presumptuous requests for add codes. They come in person: *Should I just wait till after class for an add?* And by e-mail: *Please advise on how I can get an add code.* It is one of the items on my mental checklist of first-day burdens. Deal with adds. To add or not to add? There have been times in the past when, taking the cue from other profs, I've printed up a sign to be taped on the outside of the door: NO ADDS. Some profs go the extra mile and make the poster bark: SO, DON'T ASK!

The sign on the door minimizes interruptions so that we can begin our introductory lectures on the first day of class without wasting time on the superfluous.

There have been times when I couldn't help saying out loud to the hopeful latecomers, "Why didn't you plan your schedule? Why are you scrambling around at the last minute, unprepared, foraging for open classes, begging at the eleventh hour?" And in my head, I'd continue: *Do I look like a sucker? A softy? Am I your last resort? Of course there are no adds* (with a sarcastic, Simon Cowell *Sorry!*).

Every chair is usually taken, so when I'm less possessed, I only need to gesture to the lack of seating, with or without the perfunctory apology and with an expression that says it's clearly out of my hands—a look that says, *I would if I could.*

"I don't mind sitting on the floor," they say.

"But the fire regulations prevent me from allowing that," I say.

It's all out of my hands, in other words, and it makes me feel better to know that the fire-regulation business is actually true (even though no one follows it). In fourteen years, the fire department has never knocked on my door.

On occasion, I tell them that the system simply won't let me add any more students. It's a computer thing. No way to get around it. If they knew I had the power to add, despite the lack of seating, they'd beg and plead, and try to get me to change my mind, creating a scene that quickly becomes good entertainment for the whole class. "Then can I stay and see if anyone drops?" they ask. "I'm not supposed to let anyone stay in the class unless they're enrolled," I reply. It's the played-out opening-act performance, and it runs during the first week of every semester.

Once, while I was wondering whether I needed to buckle down and cop a tougher attitude, I did just the opposite and added twenty-three students. I could; I was in the lecture hall, which holds 125 bodies, and if I maxed it out, I'd get double pay. I had 103 currently, so with the additional 23, that made 126. I thought, *I'm fine; even if one drops later, I'll still make the count.* I was adding for the money!

When a group of girls who clearly already knew each other started managing the add-code distribution process after class, I should have taken it as a clue to the kind of semester it was going to be. I had created an out-of-control monster that was destined to drag me through the muddy residue of my own greedy karma. The Buddhist metaphor of the Hell Realm came to mind. I had added too many people and would have to deal with the aftermath. Rather than passing along the sign-in sheet as instructed, after simply taking the code next to their own signature, two or three girls controlled the whole affair, divvying out codes, signing people in, and calling out names as if they were the appointed committee in charge of adding. I had been taking other questions and didn't realize what was happening until it was nearly done. I would soon discover they were part of a clique—a group of chatty friends I would have to separate all semester long. In a matter of weeks I would know each one by name, and for all the wrong reasons.

Dharma: The Lesson for Teachers

After that semester, the only thing I knew was that I would no longer allow the add-code sheet to freely circulate. The rest was up in the air.

Let's just see how it goes, Zen says.

During the subsequent semester, I wasn't in the lecture hall, and on the first day, there were already students with no seats, sitting against the wall. I hadn't put a sign on the door, and I hadn't calculated my response in advance, when I said to one guy with a skateboard under his arm, "Can't do it, man." Besides having suddenly transformed from Simon Cowell into Randy Jackson, I truly felt regretful, and despite the cluster of hopefuls that were already crowding the floor area in front of the door, I didn't want him to leave.

He understood. He understood everything and hung out at the door, vaguely nodding his head for a moment while I looked on. Some twenty seconds, or a minute, or an eternity passed before I surprised myself again by saying, "You know what—just come in, if you don't mind hangin' out on the floor for a while." There are always no-shows and drops the first week, so chairs would soon open up. He laid his skateboard and his backpack down against the wall, grateful for the spot, and turned out to be a good student.

On that day, I dealt with each inquiry that followed on an individual basis. I added only as many as I comfortably could and apologized anew to each student I couldn't add. Only one or two begged, and I empathized with their desperation. Each time, I wished I had more room. And each time, I connected with the student. Not only did the two of us feel glad as a result of the honest exchange, but the entire class felt connected as a result.

Out of habit, we tend to put limits on our capacities, but although room size might be limited, we are not. Make the commitment to meet and interact with each student separately. We walk around with a fear of connecting with one another. The connection is where the middle ground between severity and overindulgence is found. The idea of connecting sounds trite at first, but it is the work of an invisible realm, which is led by the heart rather than by speech or logic. Which is why it didn't matter whether or not the answer— the word spoken—was *Yes* or *No*. There was something more lasting and profound that was transpiring during the exchange. It's the difference between being on autopilot and tuning in. It's why, when learning to meditate or do yoga, a good teacher will remind you to follow your breath. We're so accustomed to *checking out* and remaining in a perpetual state of disconnect.

If you wake up, you can always take care
of this moment, Zen says.

Roshi says over and over, *You'll always know what to do.* And I always wondered, *How? How will I know?* Connecting with the hopeful students, even if it was just to say "No, but I'm genuinely sorry," made me feel inexplicably awake and alive as if an instant internal transformation had occurred. I felt infinitely capable of taking care of the inquiries. They suddenly didn't feel like a string of unwelcome burdens—something that should be managed, prevented, and controlled by the administration so that we can hold our classes and take care of business, thank you very much—but instead, like enthusiastic newcomers who arrived too late.

See them as friends, not interruptions. Consider how hard they have been trying to get a class. It suddenly made no difference whether it was my class, specifically, that they had sought, or whether it was *any* open class. They couldn't be more than nineteen years old! I only hoped the disappointment and first-day frustrations wouldn't turn them off to college altogether. I felt a near-maternal need to leave them with a welcoming impression of campus. I felt personally responsible and keenly aware of the fact that nobody gets priority registration their first semester.

And from my honest and direct apology, they went away with the feeling that someone was on their side, which is everything in the world. Sometimes the mere feeling of having an advocate gives life meaning, even if it is just a fleeting interaction with a stranger.

> *The difference between an ordinary person*
> *and an enlightened person is upside*
> *down thinking.*
> —Nyogen Yeo Roshi

Even if I didn't get through my introductory lecture that first day, I felt the greater value of the aliveness and the humanity of the interactions. The first day is shot, anyway, with rosters and syllabi and greetings. So why hold on to a futile agenda and the pressure to cover a certain amount of material? It will get covered. A shift in viewpoint allows us to treasure what is *meaningful* more than what is *productive* and to see the knocking inquirers as friends, not intruders. See them as gifts.

> *By helping others we help ourselves,*
> Zen says.

If I had been in danger of losing my class due to low enrollment, as many instructors were that year, each knock would have become the tap of salvation—one body closer to the eighteen necessary to hold a class open. If someone had sent me flowers, the giver would have been greeted with a blushing smile. Although our minds and preexisting attitudes shape our reactions, I came to see each inquisitor in a similar way, as a blessing, a token of their good intentions, and as a delivery of goodwill. It's like putting a face to the unseen readers of a writer's book, a fan in the singer's audience. It's my livelihood, and there's a curious mind seeking me out. His path led him to me. More than the utility of the event, though, it's a connection between the two of us. It's a chance to say, "I can't this time, but come back next semester." And they will, and they'll look forward to arriving on the first day, all because of a little smile—an interaction so small, yet bigger than a mountain and powerful enough to change hearts and minds and the world. When a stranger smiles at you, everything in the world turns sweet.

The interaction with the skateboard guy set the tone for the entire semester, and it wasn't because I covered, or didn't cover, the introductory readings.

4

The Crowd at the Door
Your Face Is Going
to Stay That Way

I never used to feel this way. I used to enjoy the banter, the interested student who would come up to me before or after class just to chat, to tell me she was enjoying the class, or, especially gratifying, to tell me how the class had inspired her or helped with a personal issue.

But this semester, maybe because I had two particularly large groups, there were always students gathered around the door, waiting for the previous class to end so they could enter early enough to get their own seats and save the neighboring chairs for their friends. I always walked up to class a few minutes early, and I would see the bodies from a distance, a signal to me that I was needed to come and inform and, moreover, to perform. Recognizing my students' faces from a short distance, I was seized by the desire to retreat, to hide myself away where I couldn't be found, where no one could ask me any questions, especially the kind that expressed confusion over the subject matter, which to my ears sounded like a challenge. *What don't you understand? Wasn't I clear enough?* Even innocuous inquiries about the date of the next test, or whether they could get another add code, seemed invasive.

It was a lecture hall, so when the previous class had finished, there would be a tidal wave of hurried bodies and backpacks spilling out of the double doors on the side of the room. In order to enter, I had to wait for the flood to hurl itself over the threshold.

After somehow weaving my way through the traffic, still maneuvering in both directions, I would install myself behind the giant desk while trying to project an anonymous air. As I emptied my bag of its contents, I was secretly hoping my presence wouldn't be taken as an open invitation for the inevitable barrage of questions and problems. At those moments, I would catch Mel, the economics professor who had the room before me, in action. I knew her only from department meetings and had found her dauntless, almost-masculine brawniness intimidating.

There was always a congested circle of impatient students pushing themselves around the long desk where she still stood, waiting their turn to convince her of their eagerness to do whatever was necessary to succeed in the class, of their readiness to research or redo, whatever had to be researched or redone. And I silently remarked on how she welcomed what I could only see as extra work, inviting them—encouraging them— to e-mail her "should there be any problems or uncertainty of any kind." She was notoriously tough and demanding, but her students rose to the challenge and strove to please her, rightfully earning their grades. She was exacting, but seemed to get results.

Dharma: The Lesson for Teachers

Protective cocoons come in many forms, from subtle sarcasm to anger and withdrawal. We often don these masks out of habit when we lack the courage to be open. Courage is often associated with aggression, but instead should be seen as a willingness to act from the heart, as reflected in the word's root. Consider both the French and Spanish sibling words for heart: *coeur* and *corazón*. The aggressive sort of courage is ego-based, while true courage asks us to lay down the ego. It starts by looking inward. Something transformative happens when we simply observe. Watching changes everything.

Paramahansa Yogananda, the great yogi and author of the beloved classic *Autobiography of a Yogi*, once told his students to *be a beacon of light that may guide shipwrecked souls.*

When you catch yourself slipping into a pool of negativity, notice how it derives from nothing other than resistance to the current situation. Notice what happens internally as a result. Conscientiously bring your attention to your face, which inevitably tightens with that resistance. Holding in mind the image of the beacon of light is to simultaneously soften the furrowed brows, the pursed lips, and the expression in your eyes. It is to open.

You shape the universe around you, Zen says.

Far from engendering a narcissistic, obsessive self-consciousness, looking inward reveals the connection between our external facade and our internal world, and further, between our demeanor and the world around us. By opening your face, you open your heart. It is as if the muscles that control both are one and the same, inextricably connected like an electronic circuit; you flip a switch on one end and the hidden surge of current flows, as if by magic, to the other.

At its most profound level, to open the heart is to start a chain of events that leads to an inevitable awakening of the spirit. To open the heart is to open into the present moment. It is to cease resisting, because resistance only takes place in the world of ideas, in the world of the mind, in the world of the past and the future, with its faraway visions of how things should be and its interminable states of longing and loathing. We resist because we have something else and somewhere else in mind, some other idea, and we prefer some other reality rather than this one.

The mere act of stopping and coming home, which starts with simply observing our state, is to come forth into the light of the present moment rather than retreat into the darkness of the mind. It is to *accept* the present moment rather than *resist* it. It is to understand that each one of us is a beacon of light that shines on everything. We affect everything we touch. It is thus to express our willingness to shine, to give, to be there. Looking inward dissolves the ego and invokes a subtle liberation that we can bring forth ourselves effortlessly.

While writing this, I had to smile at the similarity between the great yogi's teaching and something my beloved grandma used to say to me as a child. Whenever I got impatient or angry at anything, she would tell me not to "make my face ugly" because it would stay that way.

I noted another surprising similarity to the message in this chapter when I happened to catch an episode of *The Dog Whisperer* one night. In dealing with a fearful dog, Cesar Milan tried something new: He lifted up the nervous dog's tail with a leash, harmlessly holding it up while continuing their experimental walk. It had been curled and tucked between the dog's legs, but when he held the tail up like a kite, it "switched" the dog's brain from fear to confidence. It seemed like a wacky idea until it worked! It parallels the connection between our own outward facade and the state of our heart, and the power we have of affecting one with the other.

Tend to your heart and to your face as if they were one. For me, inward reflection is more immediate than looking in a mirror. I am roused by recognizing the influence of my own presence and the infinite and currently unseen effects that it would absolutely have on my young and impressionable students who have entrusted me with their ready minds. In this state of presence, burnout loses its sting and, in a very real sense, loses its meaning altogether, as in this state of presence there is nothing to resist.

There will always be students who only care about transfer units, or who enroll because their friends did, but the earnest ones are not only there to learn, but to be inspired and encouraged. And even the ones who don't care now may remember you in the future and, no matter their age, will take something away from the class— something that goes beyond the words and lectures and projects. What will your students take away? How will they remember you?

5

You're Late
Who Needs to Take
Responsibility?

When you come in late, everybody turns to see who is coming in through the door. It's just human nature; everyone's got to see. It's a reflex.

I remind my students of this silly fact on the first day of class before elaborating on the other more profound reasons not to be late. It's a matter of commitment: You signed up; you paid for it. You chose a 9:30 class because you knew you could be here at that time; you knew you'd have to leave early enough to deal with parking, and still, you decided this is a good time for you.

Most importantly, though—asking them now to find the corresponding clause on the syllabus about tardiness—it's disrespectful to others to come in late, and it's rude to me. And at that moment—when someone comes in late and everyone looks—it breaks our connection, and everyone misses what I've just said.

Through the years, as the problem continued, I added a line to the behavior section of the syllabus, noting a five-point deduction for each tardy arrival. But it still continued.

Commiserating with a colleague who teaches yoga, I learned that it happens there, too, in the confines of a yoga class, where the intent is to create an environment of tranquility. Latecomers have the gall to parade through the room, she said, trampling in front of everyone, stepping over yoga mats, water bottles, and whatever else is in their way, searching for a spot to squeeze into.

As if trying to top her, I offered that in my class, they bust through the clanging double doors in the middle of our meditation period, into a quiet, darkened room, without the sensibility or discretion to wait by the door until I hit the gong, signaling the end of our silent time. They hasten sideways through the long rows, squeezing themselves around the flipdesks while stumbling over backpacks, books, and other students' feet. And once they find a seat, they continue to shuffle around, digging through their bags in a sudden, obsessive need of a writing implement and a newfound urgency to get to work.

Sometimes the latecomers have the sense to wait by the door when they see the room is dark. But even with positive reinforcement of this courtesy, I realized at a certain point that the stumblers will still keep stumbling. They'll come right on through. And when they do, I find myself wondering, *Should I stop and make a fuss, or just ignore it and continue?* Then an agitated feeling disperses, like toxic fumes, through my face, neck, and chest. *Do the tardies represent lack of control on my part?* I ask myself. *Is that what really bothers me? Is it truly that they "disturb the peace and intimacy"?* The annoyance swells into a mushroom cloud.

They should spend a week at a Zen monastery, I think to myself. *This would never be tolerated. The bell would wake them up at 5:00 AM, and they'd be groomed and at their positions at 6:00 AM sharp. And that's here in the US where rules are lax, where even Zen monasteries cater to American comforts.*

The noxious cloud is fit to burst. *In Japan, they'd be upright on their cushions at 3:30 AM, even if they were in pain, or if they hadn't slept at all, and stragglers would never be tolerated—they'd get the stick or the boot or both. You sit through the inconveniences and the discomforts; you tolerate the cold, the hunger, and the exhaustion. And when you resist, you at least have the humility to be ashamed of your own lassitude. Here they have the privilege to go to college, and still they saunter in late without a care in the world.*

Dharma: The Lesson for Teachers

When I go to the Zen Center for Saturday service and Dharma Talk, my husband—looking for the equivalent of "Have a good time!"—calls after me to learn a lot. "I hope I *un*learn a lot," I sometimes quip in playful jest. To study Zen is to overcome ignorance. But unlike the traditional way of thinking about ignorance, as in lacking information, this particular kind of ignorance is depicted as an illusion. It is the illusory sense of separateness that reinforces negative states of mind, like anger and insult. *If I'm separate, then others must be conspiring against me.* And even though we don't articulate this aspect of the human condition in such a way, the unspoken belief underpins our chronic resentment and suspicion toward others.

The antidote for this sense of separation is to *let go* rather than accumulate. Let go of the conditioned ideas we have rather than constructing and fabricating and calculating more. Instead of stockpiling our heads with ever more ideas, the prescription is to empty and release. Release, for a moment, your perspective, your obstinacy, your certainty; in short, your own single-mindedness.

This is where *zazen,* or seated meditation, comes in. That's all Zen means—meditation—and *zazen* is at the heart of traditional Zen practice. When trying it for the first time, the first thing you'll discover is how hard it is to simply sit still. Then you'll quickly witness the unceasing flow of thoughts whirling through your head and, especially, the fact that most of them are judgment thoughts. The only point of their existence is to criticize and condemn. We slam and second-guess our own actions and those of others. We approve and disapprove of everything that flashes before our consciousness, whether it be on the inside, in the form of thoughts, or on the outside, in the form of perceptions.

Through the simple act of observation that meditation affords, the head clutter settles, like debris in a pond, leaving the water clear. The idea is that it carries over from the meditation cushion to "real life," where we can recognize the suffering that is caused by all of this finger-pointing.

Even without a formal meditation practice or commitment to Zen, you can try an experiment. Stop wherever you are and take a few moments to simply sit still. Put down the books, the phone, the coffee, and, not to be forgotten, push yourself away from the keyboard; very slowly, step away from the computer! Inevitably, you will find yourself awash in a slew of thoughts—questioning, doubting, and criticizing the way things were said and done yesterday, anticipating what might go wrong tomorrow. Simply observe the clutter, watch the endless barrage of thoughts go by, and then, the judgment that hooks itself on to each one. It is the caboose on a runaway train, calling out at every turn, Not *that* way—*this* way! Every time you find yourself judging, simply continue to observe, witness it, and perhaps even have fun with it; if you were a cartoon character, what would the bubble over your head say?

Does Zen say we're not allowed to think anything? That anything goes? That we should drift around aimlessly like zombies? Zen is often misunderstood. In contemporary culture, the term is often misused to suggest a laissez-faire attitude, such as in a conversation I overheard the other day in which one friend advised the other to forget about her gardening and lawn work, and just *be Zen about it*.

A closer look at Zen reveals a willingness to examine the previously hidden shades of reality and to enter the place where you can summon the courage to look inward, asking yourself, for example, how *you* can better inspire punctuality from your students; or, you can even consider letting it go. In my case, they are adults, in charge of their own lives, and whether or not they pay the price when they sit down to take their tests, they are too old to be spoon-fed. In addition, who knows what's going on at home. Even in the case of the younger students, a shift in perspective brings with it a willingness to surrender the protective ego-shield, the one that tries to justify our rigidity by pointing to their wrongness. Disarming ourselves in this way often exposes the farce of our own self-righteousness and presumptions. It allows us to loosen the grip we have on our own perspectives so that we can consider the possibilities that we weren't able or willing to see before.

Like those kaleidoscopes we all had as kids consider the new shapes and colors that emerge with just a small adjustment. Yes, tardiness seems intolerable, and as convinced as I am that it's a symptom of undisciplined youth, I can also laugh at myself because I'm starting to sound like the older generations who have always said the same thing. Anyway—and this is the real point—our own spinning minds that toss judgments around like batting machines are even more intolerable than the tardies. That incessant spinning ruins everything, so which is worse? They both cause suffering all around, especially to ourselves.

In his dharma talks, my Zen teacher often repeats a three-part teaching: *Don't deceive yourself; don't make excuses; and take responsibility.* Each time he transmits this message to us, he is keeping alive the flame of a living tradition, as did his own teacher, Maezumi Roshi, when he carried the very same lessons forth from his native Japan. The teachings are so pertinent that I remember them as an acronym, DER, for easy retrieval.

I always find it appealing that the teachings start with the self, putting us face-to-face with the connection between our own states of mind and our subsequent treatment of others. But looking inward at our own state of mind requires courage. *Don't deceive yourself.* How often do we mask dishonesty? It takes courage to lay the armor of the ego down and to concede—even to ourselves— our true motives and agendas. This internal candidness transforms us and, in turn, everyone and everything else we come into contact with, either directly or indirectly, which is infinite in scale over the course of a lifetime.

We go to great lengths to try to fool ourselves. I remember when I took money from my father's dresser as a kid, I told myself that if he had just given it to me in the first place, then I wouldn't have had to take it. So it was his fault. Psychologists call it *rationalizing*. A couple of years ago, my son bought a vehicle that wasn't as described in the ad. It was the first time he had handled a transaction of this magnitude on his own. He gave the seller the money and drove away with it, even though all the signs were there—no tags, an odometer reading that was higher than described, and other small peculiarities that were indications of a shady deal. Well, someone could have just stolen the tags, he said, and maybe the guy misread the mileage.

He knew he had been bamboozled, and deep down he also knew he had participated in his own deception, telling himself that it was the perfect truck—that it was a good deal, and there was no other like it. He was spellbound and ended up with undisclosed tickets and back fees on the vehicle. A good lesson, to be sure; but as adults, we're just as willing to deceive ourselves, and we get ourselves into similar situations. We do it every time we spend money we shouldn't under the guise of necessity and urgency, because the sale ends tomorrow, or because they might run out—only to look back and see we've participated in increasing our own debt. And when we're truly honest, we can see that it was for things we didn't really need.

I used to tell my students: If I had to sum up Buddhism in just one statement, I would call it the discipline of letting go. Letting go of what? The ego. The self. The *idea* of self, and the cloak of separateness the ego-self wears. Every time we deceive ourselves, we drive our ego's agenda, and we reaffirm that abiding sense of separateness. The ego is normally associated with arrogance, but that narrow definition leaves out its many other masks—such as the one it pokes through every time we refuse to budge from that avowed agenda; every time we find ourselves so rigidly attached to our own idea that we will push it at any expense—even if it means deceiving ourselves.

Student tardiness conflicts with my agenda, so my ego goes to work to control it. But as the disagreeable situation continues, the ego simmers, and the frustrated desire for control and order intensifies. I am a pressure cooker. A look, a word, or a wrong gesture opens the valve and the pressurized steam floods the room. In my head, I blame them, the culture, and the world, and it shows in my demeanor. I deceive myself by thinking I play no role in it at all, and all the while, I exhaust my energy waiting for the world to change.

When you blame, you open up a world of excuses, because as long as you're looking outside, you miss the opportunity to look inside, and you continue to suffer. Even as you employ different strategies for controlling the problem, there will always be the students that continue to trickle in late, every semester, for as long as you teach, forever. The idea of confronting yourself first, in the face of something so disrespectful, sounds ironic. *Coming in late is clearly wrong,* you may be thinking. *It's their fault, and they need to get their act together.* Yes, but you don't want to suffer until they do. You want to be liberated and at peace, able to smile as you deal with these everyday annoyances. The true irony is that when you flip the whole thing over in this way, the annoyances will probably stop being annoying. Pointing outward rather than inward prevents you from considering your own need to control and your own sensitivity to minor provocations. To continue in the context of my teacher's caveat, DER, it is thus a refusal to *take responsibility* and to take your own foibles to task.

Some of my colleagues won't admit students into the room after fifteen minutes. It's a reasonable cutoff. One of my son's teachers locks the door just one minute after the scheduled start time of his aviation class for aspiring pilots and air traffic controllers. One minute might strike you as downright unreasonable, until you hear his compelling and amusing analogy: *If this was an airplane, the doors would be locked, and even if you were only one minute late, you would have missed your plane.* Ask yourself: Where is your own balance point between "anything goes" and rigid intolerance? Curbing the compulsion to drive our agendas at any expense is part of finding that balance. And how expensive is it? Does your inner disturbance ruffle the peace more than the tardies do? If so, that is a quite a tab. Zen's answer is a compromise, which Buddha called the Middle Path.

Just watch them without controlling them, Zen says.

There's an opening of the heart that occurs when you pull back for a moment, into the stillness—when you simply watch. In that space, there is room to turn the light inward and ask honestly, "Why does this bother me so much?" Ask: is this person doing something bad to me personally? The point is not laxity, but inner peace, which has to come first. You have to be peaceful before looking to external solutions.

In the midst of the realization that a student's tardiness wasn't for the purpose of provocation, watch your reaction soften. That it's not about us, that people have their own reasons, seems obvious, yet we so often miss it. The situation might be likened to a crowded parking lot, where the tendency to come unhinged is all too easy. We've all seen tempers flare many times here, where parking spaces, time, and patience run thin. Someone takes the spot you had your eye on. You saw it first, and they just pulled right in, *Don't mind if I do*. Outrageous. But seeing the other driver's action as the result of her own pressure rather than as an affront to you personally is an example of what it means to open up into richer perspectives. To the other driver, you were just a blank face, another vehicle, just any old random car. You wouldn't have thought a thing about it if the rudeness had been directed toward the guy in front of you. Yet, when we happen to be the recipient, we take it as a personal assault, without remembering the myriad unseen possible causes underlying the rude driver's haste. Perhaps it's some pressure waiting for her at home, something dire like an abusive spouse who will grill her if she's late. Or, without too much embellishment, perhaps she's just a busy, working parent with too much to do. So, better she got that space. The point isn't to get lost in fantasy, but rather to hold up the possibility that others' actions are rarely about us, which diffuses anger and defensiveness.

We puff ourselves up and bite back out of habit, deceiving ourselves that we are under attack. In the context of DER, we could say that we utilize a handy excuse for our reactions. But greater awareness allows us to see these kinds of reactions as conditioned responses that don't serve anyone. Even if the other person was just plain old rude, the conditioned responses still don't serve— they only make things worse. Equally regrettable is that by getting sucked into our own dramas and sense of being wronged, we allow ourselves to suffer unnecessarily. And still worse is that we then unavoidably recast that negativity back out into the world in subtle countless ways.

Taking responsibility takes different forms. In some situations, it might be that an apology is in order, or it might simply be a gesture or a smile; in the parking situation, it could be a wave of the hand. Regardless of who was right, it just spreads good feelings. Taking responsibility might take the form of a simple, silent consideration that, like the fictitious, harried driver, the tardy student probably stressed all the way to class and feels terrible about being late, the way my son felt when he bought that truck.

6

The Math Major
Touchiness

As I write this, I'm supposed to have coffee next week with Farshad, an Iranian student who recently took my Philosophy in Film class. He says he brought me a souvenir from Tehran when he was back home visiting family for the holidays. He also wants to thank me for the letter of recommendation I wrote for his admission to the honors program.

He hasn't had it easy here, going through the rigors of college life in a new country without his family. Although a large number of other students on campus are also Persian, most of them were born here or brought into the country at a young age by parents who fled Iran after the Islamic revolution in 1979. There's a certain "in-crowd" feeling surrounding the dense Persian community at Santa Monica College (SMC), as most have come here together after graduating from neighboring Beverly Hills High and have known each other for many years. It was clear Farshad wasn't part of the clique.

Knowing him better now, I can surmise that his notable thinness is due to an illness that kept him in the hospital for over a month last year, one from which he has yet to recover his original weight or strength. But his frequent all-nighters—according to him, a regular part of his life, and necessary to keep up with the demands of tough courses, made even more difficult by his language struggles—contribute similarly to his frail look, as he is so consumed with his studies that he forgets to eat. And adding to his feeble appearance is a certain air particular to math majors and engineers.

I count Farshad as one of the most likable, hardworking, and sincere students I've had in my fourteen years as an instructor. Considering our tense beginnings, I never would have imagined I would think of him so warmly and that he would be counted among the handful of students I have kept in contact with after the semester's end and retained as a friend. Truth be told, after our first few meetings, I inwardly predicted he would be the bane of my existence that semester.

I remember the first time he approached me early on in the semester. It was after class on the day I had shown the first half of our first film, *The 400 Blows*.

Farshad: Why did you choose this movie?
Me: Because it relates to the topics we cover in class.
Farshad: Which topics?
Me: We haven't gotten there yet. We need to see the second half of the movie.
Farshad: But I mean, what was it about this movie that made you choose it?
Me: Aren't you enjoying it?
Farshad: I don't know. No, not really.

The exchange continued with me explaining the eventual comparison to other literary characters that have endured similar feelings of loneliness, just like the character in our film, ones that have also come face-to-face with life's precariousness. But it was an intense and disagreeable discussion, and I drove home vexed that day. I felt, in a strange way, challenged. I felt frustrated by this student, who, I imagined, must be the only one in class unmoved by the special film I hoped would stay in their minds long after the end of the semester, the way it had stayed in mine after first seeing it in college.

But Farshad continued to come to class, despite my regrettable and rather mean-spirited suggestion that the class may not be "for him" and that he was missing the beauty of the film by focusing prematurely on details. Not only did he remain enrolled, but he continued to stop by my desk after class on a regular basis. After exams, he would spend twenty minutes or more, if possible, checking and rechecking the questions he'd missed, hitting himself on the head, denouncing his stupidity for missing things he should have known. After multiple requests for undeserved grade changes in their favor from other students, I found Farshad's humility endearing.

He began to share with me things about his own background, especially his life back home, where he often felt out of place in a religiously strict and intolerant world. Once, he said he felt just like Antoine, in our very own *The 400 Blows,* or perhaps like Gregor, in Kafka's *Metamorphosis,* which we had just read alongside it. He was connecting the dots, not only thinking about the elusive topic of alienation and how it is dealt with in works of art, but also relating to our films and readings on a very personal level, and he was deeply moved by them.

We often walked out of class together after our chats. He even began to refer to himself jokingly as "Antoine," like the character in the French film he had now come to love. It turned out that he so identified with the character's numerous travails that he had come to see the beloved, timeless character as a sort of onscreen "kindred soul."

Dharma: The Lesson for Teachers

When Farshad asked, "Why did you choose this movie?" I heard something different. In my mind he was questioning my film choice and its relevance to the class.

Listen with your eyes, and
see with your ears, Zen says.

It sounds like topsy-turvy Zen talk, until you consider how complex human beings are and how important it is to listen—to really listen. Listen with your whole being. We are not the same as when we were children; our ten million life-experiences have sketched themselves onto our beings, leaving their traces as habits and tendencies, sculpting us into who we are, even as we continue to transform. *We* often don't understand why we do certain things, so it is less likely still that others, even those close to us, will be able to fathom our behavior.

But, perhaps, if we could be more generous in our willingness to perceive, if we could see with our ears and listen with our eyes, it would reduce the misunderstandings that wedge us apart in a fog of suspicion and resentment.

When we feel criticized, our defense mechanisms spring into action. But it is the small mind, better known as the ego, that worries about approval. When this fearful little self starts to shout, compassion is impossible, since compassion requires a big-enough mind with which to see and a big-enough heart with which to receive. Without this spirit of openness, there is no communication. There is only attachment to one's perspective.

The great Indian yogi, Paramahansa Yogananda, once spoke about the problem of touchiness. It is the corollary of an untamed ego, resulting in an inferiority complex. It rightly mirrors the Buddhist teachings on the problem of the ego, as Buddha himself was a Raja yogi, steeped in the same timeless Indian wisdom that Paramahansa Yogananda, Gandhi's spiritual teacher, brought to the West less than a century ago.

Touchiness is the tendency to be oversensitive and to feel easily offended. The wise yogi referred to it as a nervous habit that can only destroy peace, as we rise to defend ourselves in various ways each time we feel hurt. Some people brood silently, while others bite back with harsh words and counterattacks. This is the root of most arguments and misunderstandings between people, no matter what kind of relationship they share. Buddha was concerned with the problem of human suffering, and touchiness creates abundant suffering within oneself and in others. The touchy person, feeling wronged, suffers inner torment while making the supposed offender suffer in return.

I was touchy with Farshad. When we look back, we often don't understand what could have pushed our buttons so easily. With a greater willingness to perceive, I might have seen his probing questions not as complaints or challenges but as a reflection of his need to mathematically analyze whatever he's presented with and to create a bulleted outline in his notes. He couldn't help it; it's part of who he is.

Of course, not everyone will like every movie that's shown in class, but this one is my personal favorite, which means that I'm attached to it and expect that the class will love it just as much. I also see my film class as a respite where I get to share treasured classics. In my eyes, an overanalytical math major who "misses the forest for the trees," as I embarrassingly insinuated, diminishes the magical atmosphere I hope to create.

Such is the problem with agendas. They'll never be met.

Farshad and I taught each other. He confessed to missing, at first, the beauty of the Truffaut classic, only to discover it as we went on. And I saw that greater insight on my part would have afforded me more patience for his personality. It would have allowed me to see through the qualities in his character that I found disagreeable at first, because seeing through the myriad things in people that alternately attract and repulse is to simultaneously go beyond the trappings of our desires and our will to make everyone be the way we want them to be. Like the yogi who pulls the scorpion up out of the water time after time, even after it continues to bite him, I would have been able to help him connect the mathematical dots and symbols, which was all he wanted. I would have spoken words that he could hear.

Cultivate a willingness to listen more deeply. Listen with your eyes, and see with your ears. Wrongful perception exacerbates touchiness and the resentment that hangs on the shadow of misunderstandings. And when it does happen, and it inevitably will, make amends.

After arguments, most of us stew in a thick broth of rancor and resentment, repeating the dialogue and rehearsing for the next scene, when we can tell the other person how right we were and enumerate all the points on which they were wrong. My Zen teacher recently told a story about his own teacher, the revered Taizan Maezumi Roshi, and a dispute they once had. Shortly after the disagreement, they happened to pass one another on the grounds outside the monastery, and the smiling Japanese Zen master simply said, slowly and softly, with the sweetest downward lilt, and with complete absence of ill humor, "Hi, Nyogen." My teacher grumbled to himself, "Bah . . . I'm still in demonmode . . . don't talk to me." My teacher shared his memory with us during one of his weekly dharma talks. He wanted us to remember the importance of coming back to center, with no lingering irritation, just like his teacher did. Sometimes this is all it takes to make things right.

7

Grading Papers
There Is No Beginning and No End

Why do I assign this work? I ask myself as I contemplate the stack of papers that sits indiscreetly on my desk. As I scan the towering mountain of work to be done, the familiar wave of resistance swells up. *Why do I do this to myself?* I continue the monologue. I can't avert my gaze. I won't be at ease until they're graded, yet I push them away, buying just one more day, and suddenly I'm a kid again, staring at the heap of soggy squash on my plate, recoiling at the sight of it.

There they are, right in the middle of my desk, gathered into a neatly packaged, puffed-up bundle, distorting the blue plastic sleeve that contains them. Self-satisfied and engorged, I hear their mock greetings: *Well, top o' the mornin' to you! Pretty big stack, eh?* Besides having taken on an Irish identity and a condescending sneer, the stack of papers has grown bigger and taller than Mount Kilimanjaro. Their placement on my desk is strategic; an unavoidable confrontation takes place here first thing every morning when I come to check my e-mail, which makes forgetting about them impossible. They're almost finished, I lie, when my students ask anxiously if I've graded their papers—their 125 papers. *Did you like mine?* one asks, thinking that teachers can't wait to curl up with a big, thick stack of papers and mark them all up.

Dharma: The Lesson for Teachers

The true irony is that once I start, the counting will stop. Avoidance only brings discontent. Who lures me into this game of cat and mouse, where I'm the mouse and the overstuffed envelope staring back at me is the cat? I do. Led by my imagination—a fanciful thing by nature—and appalled by the denseness of the bundle, I convert it into a towering beast, my adversary, with whom I must do battle.

Although the papers are very much a reality, resisting them turns them into a fictitious thing, an image that takes on a life of its own. As soon as we get lost in our mental images, we lose our presence. It is an indulgence that keeps us stuck in our heads, where we drift like an unmoored fishing boat, bobbing into the past and then the future, meandering through a fantasy world that doesn't actually exist. In this distorted version of reality, we fabricate expectations along the way of how things will be when we get there. We even distort the past. The result is a life stuck in this homespun fantasy world—but it's not the kind of fantasy world where dreams come true. Rather, it's a nightmare of a place infested with visions and expectations, and because the event is never like the vision, we end up plagued with chronic delusion and, in turn, persistent disappointment and frustration.

Tourists are often disappointed with their vacations because while they were planning them and shopping for all the right clothes, they were envisioning something different. We used to tease my dear grandmother because of the abundance of food she would prepare at get-togethers, having envisioned everyone voraciously devouring seconds, and thirds, and fourths, along with huge masses of pie, endlessly pouring, slicing, and grabbing. Students procrastinate when it comes to writing their papers because in their mind's eye, their simple written summary has become a hundred-page dissertation. And dieters give up because twenty pounds seems too daunting.

But right here, there's only one dish! And one page, and one pound.

Although the outcome is sometimes amusing, such as my grandma's holiday spreads, the tendency to get stuck in fantasies often has a stymieing effect. Guided by the vision of a mountain to climb, a track to complete, or twenty pounds to lose, we plod continually forward with an eye toward advancement—not merely advancement, but the big finish . . . the day when we'll have *gotten there.* When we're in school, one eye is fixed on graduation, and after graduation, we set that same eye on the job of our dreams, and once we achieve that, we're already bored and planning our next vacation. Soon, we're anticipating retirement, when we can be free of it all. Then we'll wish we were young again. And we live that way because in our visions, there is always a mountain to climb. Yet in real life, mountains are never climbed. Steps are taken.

I remember the first time I sat a retreat. The idea of sitting for another hour—the seventh one spent on the cushion that day— seemed absolutely undoable. *One more hour? These people are all crazy!* I thought to myself. An hour is a long time, but only if you continually think about it, since, when you're thinking about it, you're not doing it wholly, whatever it is. You're then separated from the activity and from time itself. Nobody has ever sat for an hour. It's an arbitrary division of space-time to help us make sense out of it. It's an abstraction that warps with our experiences. You only sit one flashing, unnamable moment at a time.

My introduction to Zen was through the writings of Alan Watts, who used to explain that there's only ever one dish to wash. I was a freshman in college and ended up with my first Watts book, of many more to come, when I was tutoring a friend in algebra. She said it had been her dad's book and she had no use for it. I was intrigued by the puzzling promise of the title, *The Wisdom of Insecurity*. It all comes back to presence. In our minds, we turn the sink full of dishes into an enormous thing; we can all relate to seeing the crowded sink and not knowing where to even start. It's like the gargantuan tower of papers I have to grade—125 of them—a seemingly unfeasible number. But like time itself, it is an abstraction. Numbers become ideas in our minds and reside there in the mythical realm of the future.

There is no beginning and no end, Zen says.

When I first started doing *zazen,* or Zen meditation, as part of my formalized training, my teacher told me to count my breath, and as everyone else does when they start, I raced to get to the number ten, as if I would win some big prize for getting there quickly. While nearly hyperventilating one day, I realized how silly it was to rush to ten. Where is it we want to go? And where will we go after ten? Back to one again, of course! It is what the beloved Zen master Shunryu Suzuki meant when he said that there is no such thing as "this afternoon." He meant that we could only do one thing at a time.

We're rushing to our deaths, Zen says.

We go through life forever trying to get to ten. We look to the clock with great expectations, forever asking, even as grown-ups, *if we're there yet.* We humor the children when they ask, but we ask too, in our own rushed ways, in all the days of our lives, and in everything we do, forever rushing to the end. The end of what? If this continues throughout every activity, throughout the rest of our lives, the only end in sight is death.

As an experiment, catch yourself the next time you find yourself thinking in terms of quantity. It might be the day's errands, or the pile of bills, or, like me, the talking stack of papers on your desk. Simply notice the feeling of urgency and the tendency to rush through them. Notice, also, the inclination to shrink back. Although they seem like opposite tendencies, both come from the same feeling of aversion and serve only to keep us out of touch with the actual task. We're taken aback by the enormity of what we've created in our minds, so we say, *I'm just going to plow through it and get it done*, or, *It's too overwhelming and I don't know where to start.* See them both as nothing more than habits that come from our skewed way of envisioning time.

Both responses pull us out of the freshness of direct experience. They both bind us to the fantasy of a task rather than the reality of it, warping our sense of what is really required. Wasting energy on head trips is exhausting, and we do it to ourselves. A task is done in steps, because reality is made up of steps, infinitely divided flashes of time that are too small to measure. We come to life and our energy soars when we join that moment, rather than standing separate from it—when we rise to the occasion rather than sink into the pit of resistance. When we join the moment, we join time. We are time.

Ultra distance runner Pam Reed understands this. When running superhuman distances that require her to continue on for three days straight, with no sleep or breaks of any kind, she tells herself she only has to get to the next pole, to the next marker, right *there*. She keeps herself from getting vacuumed up into the enormity of the distance and ends up at the final mark by employing these little tricks—which are less like tricks than they are reminders of reality itself.

Time is an abstraction that stops and stares right back at us as soon as we separate ourselves from it. To be separated from time is to watch it. It's a shy child that can't play naturally and acts awkwardly when we watch, but as soon as we look away and rejoin our conversations, she continues to play naturally. Time flows when we stop watching it. Staring at the clock is to resist reality. *I don't like this situation—can't this clock move any faster!* Like Pam Reed, we need only put one foot in front of the other and take a step right here and now.

"But," you may ask, "does this mean that Zen, with all its talk of *the now*, scoffs at imagination?" We have all been taught as kids to be imaginative; artists have been taught to be imaginative. It's not for nothing that we celebrate the gift and splendor of imagination. But like all good tools, it has its place. After all, the creative process itself unfolds in real time.

Think of the jazz improv artist responding to the musical banter among her fellow players onstage. Aside from whatever training they've done in advance, as soon as the curtain opens, they move into unknown territory together, creating something new each time by remaining in a state of undivided presence. They let go of their ideas and preconceptions of how it should be, how they thought it was going to be, and how other musicians have done it in the past. They let go of their agendas and simply move together in the flow, with the faith that comes from experience, trusting in their own abilities as artists and in each other.

It may help the sports star, too, to envision his plays in advance, but if he doesn't remain in a state of absolute presence when the time comes to execute the play, he'll miss the ball. He plays the real game in real time.

Imagination, like intellectualization, is put away when it has done its job. The imaginative vision provides a palette of possibilities, which are then actualized in a state of presence and, ironically, with the willingness to let go of the expectations of the vision. To paraphrase my Zen teacher, there's nothing wrong with imagination, so long as it hasn't got you by the nose.

How do you release the mind of its time-warped visions? By releasing them. And when the mind is clear of the mountains of fantasies, where do you start? You just start.

"If I am so busy planning how to eat next week that I cannot fully enjoy what I am eating now, I will be in the same predicament when next week's meal become now."

—Alan Watts, *The Wisdom of Insecurity*

8

Illiteracy
Forgive

I don't know why I should feel embarrassed when I try and explain the depths of the grammar problem that exists at the college level. I teach philosophy, not English. Besides, the problem is bigger than just one teacher. Nonetheless, this dilemma takes the form of a guilty conviction that as long as I'm passing my students along, I'm passing the buck. I am one more teacher in a string of countless others they've had along the way that were well-meaning but either too soft-hearted, too overwhelmed, or too burned-out to clamp down on the problem of illiteracy.

I used to be surprised when I'd see "there" instead of "their" repeatedly—not a onetime typo, but repeatedly throughout the body of a major writing assignment. But it's so common, I don't even lift an eyebrow anymore. My eyes used to bulge at the mix-up between "its" and "it's," or at the sight of basic verb conjugations having run amok. I used to think it was basic fourth-grade stuff.

When I was little, my grandmother had me convinced that using the word "ain't" was on the same level as murder. It was a crime. An unutterable sin. Like so many other immigrants in her day, my grandma was anxious to speak good English and assimilate into the American culture. She was proud when she became a schoolteacher. I wonder what she would think if she were still alive and happened to see the papers I regularly receive, with "ain't" strewn around like little scraps of unwanted litter (and often without the modest dignity of an apostrophe).

If I turn my back on the problem and leave it alone, everyone will simply go on their way. "What a fun class," they'll say. But there's a voice inside me that recoils at the thought and remonstrates against such a world. Maybe it's my grandma's voice. It's the voice that says illiteracy is inexcusable, and that presses on, saying, *How can I just ignore it?* and, *What will become of the next generation?* Especially when it's not just one or two problem kids—it's the majority of the class.

But then I ask, *What's the point?* The system is defective, and I can't fight the system. It didn't get that way overnight, and it isn't due to just one simple, fixable cause. A thousand traceable and untraceable, intertwined causes have created the misshapen entity we call *the system.* Lack of funding and overcrowding throughout schools at every level are but a few of the reasons. Political correctness, with its misappropriated idea of *tolerance*—which never meant *anything goes*—is also part of the problem as it inhibits some teachers from making necessary corrections. And text-messaging—where clipped words are now the norm for kids whose experience with any other kind of writing is limited—contributes to the declining respect for language and is but one of the many seen and unseen roots of a dysfunctional system.

Many teachers create activity classes where nobody has to write anything. As a teacher, I understand why. Meanwhile, though, we're matriculating partially illiterate young adults all the way through the system. By the time I get them, in community college, bad habits are hard to break, yet still, after their two years of general education, many will transfer over to a four-year university. The irony is that while university standards are tougher, the quality of work and literacy is lower. To let it slide and not deal with this hidden blemish in our schools makes me feel like a hypocrite. But with overcrowded classes across the board, and no funding in sight for teachers' aides, our options are limited.

As one individual teacher, I could choose to simply overlook the horrendous sentences—because, after all, it's an Asian Philosophy class, not an English class—or I could heroically stop them in their tracks and let them know they are not writing at the college level. I could refuse to pass them along. What stops many instructors from doing just that is the messy aftermath. The inevitable barrage of e-mails at the end of the term, the storm of grade petitions, the mass of complaints that already come in healthy numbers, because without a near 4.0 GPA on their transcripts, they'll be denied entry into universities. Bs are no longer good enough, with the overcrowding and underfunding that has forced universities to tighten up their admissions policies. When students come to me complaining about their Bs, I always tell them that when I was in school, Bs were considered good grades.

I can overlook the mess on the papers in front of me because the damage has already been done—it's been done for years, and it's not likely one person can change the widespread and deeply engrained deficiency. So, I think to myself, why fight it and willfully bring the suffering upon myself and my class? It's reasonable, I say, to simply throw down the gauntlet and give alternative assignments, ignoring the twinge of inner shame that says I'm sloughing off my duty.

Those who get to the point where they choose to let it go, to overlook the situation, often opt to replace written exams with multiple-choice versions to be taken on Scantron forms. A colleague described the instance when she implored her class to get help. It was on a Monday, after spending the whole weekend grading, "like an English teacher." She gave them a speech, reminding them that many of them will be teaching children one day, themselves, and that it is important, as teachers, to have a reasonable command of the language. She asked them, without an ounce of rhetoric, what they will teach our children if they don't at least obtain a basic grasp of the language. She concluded her speech by requesting them to visit the tutoring center, where free help is readily available. The result was that one person got help.

Dharma: The Lesson for Teachers

Expect less from your relationship and more from yourself.
                                        —Karen Maezen Miller

Turning the pointer inward rather than outward doesn't imply, by any means, that we are shirking the needs of our relationships. Quite the contrary. Looking inward is a gesture that conveys our willingness to confront our own role in life's unfolding series of events and in what we interpret as problems. Although originally given in the context of family relationships, the charge to expect more from ourselves can be applied to any situation. Ask yourself, for example, how you can expect less from the class and more from yourself. Although at first it may sound like an excuse to walk away from the challenge at hand—in this case, literacy—it is an invitation to discover hidden perspectives, new approaches, and unforeseen solutions.

It's a matter of seeing things through a different lens and summoning up the courage to let go of the assumptions, the beliefs, and even the guilt that are all indelibly etched into our minds. Prominent among them is the abiding belief that we have to fix everything outright and the adjoining reflex that we have to do something. We feel we have to *do* something about every perceived rough patch—that we have to correct every wrong.

> *It's the picking and choosing mind,*
> Zen says.

Next time you feel strongly about the wrongness of a certain situation, try an experiment. Instead of acting on it right away, consider whether your concern is simply the offshoot of some personal attachment or aversion—what is known in Zen as *the picking and choosing mind* at work. Bravely confronting ourselves this way doesn't mean we're passing the buck.

Sometimes we don't realize how things will look the other way until reality has been flipped around for us. For example, in the movie *The Soloist,* when Jamie Foxx's homeless character is generously presented with his own apartment, his response is surprising: "Don't box me in, inside, away from the world, away from life!" It is surprising because it is contrary to the way we usually think. We are conditioned to look upon a domicile as necessary shelter, as covering from the elements, as a place of retreat and protection from the chaos and dangers of the streets. But his character, based on a real-life person, only saw entrapment. He saw walls that locked him away from the world and into an unnatural, prison-like confinement. People said he was the crazy one, but once we flip our perspective, it becomes easier to see things the way he saw them. To him, we're the dysfunctional ones—cut off from life, tucked away inside these walls of separation we call houses.

Consider those written assignments, all so appalling and lacking in basic proficiency. If I could turn the viewfinder on myself, I might gaze into my own arrogance and judgmental tendencies, which are foibles that equal my students' own. This change of perspective requires more effort and honesty, but the reward is immense, carrying with it the potential to affect far more than your immediate relationships and circumstances. Yes, as teachers, it's our job to grade our students' work, but there's this invisible marvel going on that is ever more powerful than any mark we could ever make on their papers. Your students imbibe your manner and transmit it through their own interactions, touching and influencing others in ways you can't fathom, any more than you could foresee the eventual effect of an earthquake on the ocean at large. Your way with them totally eclipses anything else. This inner redress engenders a wider perspective that subdues the tendency to see students as the sole culprits and simultaneously brings about a state of ease that ripples outward indefinitely.

Although admittedly, this tendency still comes up, I have come to see my overattentiveness to their writing as just another personal aversion that I was camouflaging in the cloak of righteousness. Pema Chodron tells a story about her disappointment in a student who fell off the wagon and started using drugs again. Her spiritual teacher, the honored Trungpa Rinpoche, told her to drop her expectations with regard to others' behavior and to just be kind to them. He encouraged her to help them move slowly forward by way of her own kindness and to bring a little happiness into their lives. He said that "setting goals for others can be aggressive!"

In Trungpa's tradition, this commitment to inner transformation is known as the Warrior Path. The toughest warrior act of all is confronting yourself, but when we call ourselves out on our own fears, aversions, and attachments, something transformative happens not only on the inside, within ourselves, but on the outside, among others, as well.

When I mentioned the situation of illiteracy to my own spiritual teacher one day, his response went straight to the heart of it like an arrow. He spoke of the importance of knowing your limitations, knowing what you can and can't do, and knowing how you can best be of service. Even Mother Teresa knew she couldn't clean up all of Calcutta, he said. But she *could* help individuals one at a time. It was an aha moment for me. It shattered the vague and unarticulated idea I'd had, that unless something was done on a large scale, it wouldn't matter. Where should you put your efforts in order to best be of service? As teachers, a creative, personalized response is clearly more transformative than the stifled rage provoked by badly written term papers.

There is no singular answer to the problem of illiteracy, but we can ask different questions. And through asking, new perspectives are inevitably revealed. The rain is either miserable or cozy, depending on your outlook and mood. It is your perspective that reveals new possibilities. In the classroom, it is often the students themselves that reveal them.

Many students aren't writing at an appropriate level, but ask them what they *are* good at. Many draw well, or sing well, and most are technologically savvy. Many are compassionate and are involved in philanthropic activities. Many have, for example, taken on elder care or have assumed the responsibilities of sibling care. Others are involved in environmental activism and have pioneered their own modern-day grassroots movements. I wish I had some of their skills and motivation. What should be the standard? Which skill is the most highly prized? Our own values, which are shaped by our attachments and aversions—by *the picking and choosing mind*—determine our answer to those questions.

And that's the point. Because I personally value language, I attach importance to it. It is a bias. What are your attachments, and how have they shaped your teaching? Going further, what has shaped the attachments themselves? Innumerable causes. In this instance, culture as a whole, with its inflexible canon of standards and measures, has, without our even being aware of it, impacted what we consider valuable.

As an aside, this is part of what is wrong with standards-testing throughout our entire educational system, with its requisite barrage of SATs, GMATs, LSATs, and all the other tests that focus only on outcome, without any means of recognizing the many shades of value and the many brands of intelligence and talent that are latent inside each individual student.

The most precious gift to me is when students tell me how the class has transformed their lives in some way. Sometimes they ask for advice, and sometimes I'm able to give it, even if it's just a few words of encouragement. It's gratifying when they later visit me or send me an e-mail just to let me know the advice did help or that the class inspired a new approach to some other challenge. Those are the moments that make teaching rewarding. Next time you experience that same rewarding feeling, ask yourself, isn't this the good stuff?

In practical terms, there are infinite alternative methods of testing, and I make no pretense of fixing the system. But in the interim, what we can change is our perceptions, which have the effect of changing everything. When you receive your students' written work, hold in your mind the oft-forgotten fact that progress arrives in stages. Remember that sometimes the steps are small and we may miss them, just as we never really see our kids growing up, or ourselves growing old—we only see it in retrospect. Remembering this is to remember the middle ground; it's not a case of writing well or failing. While continuing to encourage better communication skills and higher literacy levels, we can remind ourselves of the supreme importance of improvement. It's not all about outcome. Keeping in mind the advice Pema Chodron's teacher gave her, we can remember our role as one of many teachers who will all have a hand in helping them advance gently one step at a time, rather than aggressively trying to transform them wholly in accordance with our own values, goals, and agendas all at once.

9

Sit like a Big Boy
Oneness

He had his legs draped over his girlfriend. But, as I later learned, she was not his girlfriend; they were just flirting. It was impossible not to stare, not only because they were right in front of where I stand to lecture, right in front of the two center aisles, but because he had to lift his legs for any latecomer who needed to pass through, as if he was in kindergarten, playing London Bridge.

One day, after ceaseless teasing and play-fighting between the two of them, I moved them both. All I had to do was point to be understood, and they stumbled with their backpacks and loose belongings toward the only two empty seats by the wall. As they were settling into their new places, Tim hit his head on the overhanging television and commenced exaggerated grimacing while rubbing his head to demonstrate his injury. Then, with all eyes still locked on him, unavoidably following his every action, he continued to hold his head for another minute or two, maintaining his contorted expression of pain as I stood there, waiting to lecture. I knew that any look of sympathy on my part would only have encouraged his performance. I eventually moved them again, separately.

An attorney friend, trained to look for motives, asked me once if I could tell whether the perpetrators in class were disturbing me on purpose or not. Here was a kid who, despite his childish displays, managed to evoke my good humor. One day while lecturing, I noticed he was twisted over to the side, ostensibly digging for something in his backpack and, again, chatting in spurts with the girl that was not his girlfriend. I told this nineteen-year-old college student to "sit like a big boy." Later, when he put his head down quietly for a moment, I couldn't help reaching over and scratching his head as if he were a dog.

He pushed his limits when he started up with his juvenile antics right in front of the camera one day when my lecture was being filmed. He was chuckling at his own secret jokes and simultaneously texting on his cell phone. All I had to do was display incredulity on my face, along with an unrehearsed, audible whisper: "Oh, you're *not!*" He put his phone away in a hurry, even though it didn't take long before he was texting again as if he just couldn't help himself.

In the future, all it took was what my son used to call the "mommy eyes" or a quick shaking of my head to snap him out of these derailments. He gave me a thank-you card, some suntan lotion (which I didn't question), and a hug at the end of the semester, and we wished one another happy holidays.

Dharma: The Lesson for Teachers
For countless reasons, the infatuated nineteen-year-old either revels in—or yearns desperately for—attention; in addition, you can

almost smell the hormones wafting around his whole person like a perfume cloud. An attention-seeking boy who is also infatuated makes an ebullient mix; it's like putting too much leavening in the cake batter. The other kids were sitting still, but to compare him with the rest of the class would be to ignore the ten thousand unseen threads that weave themselves into the fabric that composes our varied personalities. Caring for each in the same cavalier way may be easier, but heedless. As any mother knows, even in the context of one small family, each child has her own character with her own unique needs. Some need more patience than others; others, more tenderness; and others, more guidance. How much more so in a classroom of over a hundred random kids of varying ages! I used to think the classroom was different—that in this neutral space, my rules would be my rules, and that would be that.

If my lawyer friend were to put me on trial for this incident, I could answer with conviction that Tim's motives lacked maliciousness. He wasn't challenging me. His behavior wasn't about me at all. That's the bottom line: It never is. That's the point of compassion, which is not the same as sympathy. And the difference lies in overcoming ignorance, which is not the same as stupidity. The bigger challenge is extending the engulfing warmth of compassion to everyone, which is not the same as lenience. It is our willingness to open up to kinship with all beings and to consider our unity, regardless of whether it feels easy or hard.

When the Buddha spoke of ignorance, he was referring to the false sense of separation between us. The suggestion that the separation between things is spurious, that it's somehow not real, sounds not only counterintuitive, but so strange and unfathomable that it's just easier to ignore the whole idea. It's as if someone just told you aliens were coming to land downtown today.

When the yogis and the seers from ancient times allowed us a stolen glimpse into their mystical experience, they revealed their wordless insights through metaphor. They pointed the way with poetry, song, or, like the holy men of the desert, through spinning dance. They whispered of the unity behind appearances, pointing out that the separateness we perceive is all a mask, a bewitching illusion, which in the end is only fool's gold.

Using a contemporary metaphor, it would be like the interface of any computer program, website, or even your Facebook page—all the links and pictures and novelties merely colorful masks covering the nexus of electric current underneath, reducible still to strings of mathematical data incomprehensible to most of us.

There is no separation, Zen says.

Seeing through this illusion is what it means to overcome ignorance, or the false sense of separation between us, and it is this insight and sense of connection that brings forth a natural feeling of compassion. It is to enter into *oneness.* But seeing through the fog takes genuine effort. All spiritual disciplines pointing the way to the same state of clarity can offer only tricks, ways to wipe the windowpane, so that we can get at least a peek. We have to apply ourselves sincerely through various forms of practice. One form is to simply consider our mutual dependency and shared experiences.

There's an old Tibetan training technique that serves just this purpose and is used to cultivate universal compassion. Unlike the preferential sympathy that we normally associate with the word *compassion*, true compassion spirals outward naturally from the tuned-in mind, the mind that penetrates the dusty surface where we get trapped in the features that either attract or repel us. Sympathy is based on attachment to someone or something in particular, whereas compassion is like a beam that illuminates the sameness in all of us.

Following the Tibetan training instructions, try to imagine that all beings were, at one time or another, during some past lifetime, your mother. It breaks through the barrier of animosity that prevents us from extending compassion to those whose motives we don't trust or who have been unkind to us. Imagining a mother's lovingkindness is a powerful aid when done with concentration. Like the heat of the first summer sun, when applied wholeheartedly, it can melt the icy barrier of judgment and animosity.

If the Tibetan meditation feels too intangible, with its presumption of reincarnation, you might feel more at home with my own variation. Try imagining that the person nearest you may, in some strange and unforeseeable future disaster, be the person who saves your life. Next time you're in a situation that tries your patience, imagine the gratitude you'd extend toward that same person you first found annoying. This is even more powerful when applied in the classroom—although it is more difficult because it requires mentally suspending the illusion of power and invincibility that we wear in the classroom as teachers. In this variation, the would-be lifesaver is a student—a kid who, for example, rushes in without hesitation to pull you up when you've fallen.

Where the traditional Tibetan method asks you to imagine that the unlikable person *was once* helpful, in the past, this version asks you to imagine that the difficult person *might be* helpful in the future. Both have the effect of diffusing the shield of alienation between us.

Once, as part of my yoga teacher-training, I went to a master class in an overcrowded, overheated studio where everyone's mats were already touching, and I knew there would be no room to simply open our arms in many of the poses. When I walked in, they had to make room for me in the back. I was no longer embarrassed when yet two more people squeezed themselves in after me, and despite the open, spiritual intent of advanced practitioners, the vexation was palpable each time we had to scoot. The teacher joked about how common it is at the beginning of a crowded class to feel aversion toward whoever happens to be next to you, to dislike the fact that he's even there, and to dislike everything about him: his pants, his face, and even his water bottle. But by the end of class, everyone is a friend, and everyone is hugging one another good-bye with genuine warmth and sincerity.

We are difficult creatures. Why do we have to wait until the end of class to be friends? I've watched a similar phenomenon unfold in my own academic classes. No one talks to anybody else until test day. But on that day of the first test, I always enter to the chirping and buzzing of friendly chatter that fills the room—or perhaps, it's the nervous chatter of commiseration that psychologists refer to as *affiliation*. Nonetheless, it is an act of bonding that ensues under certain circumstances, revealing our solidarity and shared experiences.

That day in the yoga studio, I ended up next to a young man who couldn't have been more than twenty-two years old. He was dripping with sweat just inches away from me. During one of the balancing pose sequences, he lost his footing and started to fall backward, right into me, but I reached up and caught him, supporting him by the shoulder until he regained his balance. We smiled at each other, both knowing a sweaty, bell-ringing blow had been averted, and then we simply continued our practice, with the invisible partition of personal space now completely dissolved.

Although the word *compassion* sounds mushy, it is the natural result of removing the barriers that the protective ego has constructed as protection. In my classroom and in the yoga studio, circumstances hastened their removal, leaving a space that kindheartedness could fill. Imagine if this all-encompassing, indiscriminate flow could burst forth spontaneously. It would flood the room, washing over everyone equally without regard to personal preference or circumstance and without having to be twisted out of us.

Compassion allows us to fathom the myriad reasons behind other people's behavior and our own similar behavior. As a fun memory experiment, think back to when you were the same age as your students. Did you ever doze off in class, send notes back and forth to a friend, or stare at someone you had a mad crush on while class was going on all around you? I cringe as I recall the long-buried, countless ways I wasted time in class and aggravated my teachers when I was young. Remembering is not to condone any of it—it's to bring ourselves to the state of equanimity, of calm compassion, where we can then proceed more effectively. Compassion is knowing that we, too, have been there. It's to at least hold up as a possibility some of the various perspectives that compose any story. It's to get past our barriers, and most importantly, ourselves.

Getting past ourselves means getting past our egos. Ordinarily thought of as arrogance, in its subtler shades, ego is desire, attachments, expectations. It is greed. It is the *picking and choosing mind*. It is jumping to conclusions, clinging to positions, single-minded stubbornness. It is anger. It is *pushing your agenda*. And it is all grounded in fear. The ego is the insecure part of us that needs constant recognition, approval, reassurance, and flattery (of which there is never enough). Mostly, ego just needs to be right. It is ignorance. It is *the dualistic mind*. And because of the fear generated by its exaggerated sense of self, and because of its dogged fixation on meeting its needs, it is in a constant state of alienation, worry, and suspicion of others' intents. When these pestilent mental states are painstakingly peeled away layer by layer, the light of compassion shines through, and we find that in this new state of lightness, we are able to harmonize with our surroundings, enabling others to effortlessly harmonize with us.

"No thoughts are moving around, there is just the flame of
awareness. In this state the observer is no longer separate from the
observed, the knower is no longer separate from the known, the
hearer is no long separate from the speaker. In that moment these
is the communication; in that moment there is the transfer. Then,
anything will do, my world will do, any gesture of my hand will do."

—Osho, *Zen: The Path of Paradox*

10

Three-Way Eye Tag
Pushing the River Puts You in Over Your Head

I was teaching in a lecture hall with two large sections of seats separated by a horizontal passageway running through the center. Two girls always sat next to each other in the first row of the back section. During one of the multiple-choice exams, I watched as one of the girls looked repeatedly at the other's exam. I wanted to confirm my suspicion of cheating before moving her. Would she try to steal answers from her friend's Scantron form with me watching her? I had 125 other pairs of eyes to watch, yet I kept going back to hers.

When I was a graduate student, I had heard about a Chinese geography professor who would stand on his own large desk, looming over his students while they tested, so as to preclude the possibility of cheating. I never took a class with him, but his legend, albeit a bit humorous, left me in dismay of his lack of trust in adult-age students, who I assumed were long past the babysitting age.

Gullible as it sounds, during my first few years as an instructor, I never considered the possibility that any of *my* college students would cheat. That changed forever one day; I had merely stepped outside the room for a moment to chat with another professor while a few remaining students lingered over their exams. One young woman, feeling obliged to tell me the truth, came out and whispered, *The guy in the back just went up to your desk and totally copied answers from the stack of completed exams piled up there!* Apparently, he had stood there, plain as you please, copying answers while feigning to turn in his own. My bubble of naiveté was burst, collapsing my trust in an instant.

I remembered the Chinese professor and sympathized with his old-fashioned surveillance system. The next day, in a moment of uncanny synchronicity, I received a faculty e-mail warning of the campus-wide problem of cheating. Since then, I have had to employ tighter vigilance over my students while they test rather than doing some casual reading or beginning to correct the exams at my desk as I used to do. Since becoming a warden, I've often had to move shady-looking suspects—with their wandering eyes and suspicious positions—to seats that are easier to monitor. The fact that relocating students was not new to me anymore made it all the more strange that I hadn't immediately moved the girl with the wandering eyes.

Too much time had now passed while engaged in what I can only refer to as a strangely compelling game of eye tag. I felt like it was too late to move her, as if inertia had rendered it impossible. We were stuck in a monotonous and repetitive routine of exchanging glances. Breaking out of the silent entanglement would now seem ridiculous after catching so many "accidental" glimpses of each other. She was stealing looks to her right and then at me, to see if I had seen her, and I was watching her, making sure she knew I *had* seen her, because if she knew I was watching, she wouldn't dare satisfy my suspicion by really stealing an answer, would she? And she wouldn't, couldn't, stop looking toward her right because stopping would be an admission of guilt. So for her, it was better to simply continue the casual sideways glances, looking as nonchalant as possible.

Every time another student unwittingly interrupted this silent game with a whispered question about the test, my paranoia intensified, since with my attention diverted, she would surely get her stolen answers. I silently willed the interrupter to accept my dismissive response and go away quickly. Later, I felt cheated out of the satisfaction of attending to those questions with more interest and attention.

I finally relaxed when both girls' tests were turned in, making a mental note of their names so I could later compare their scores. Both tests were identical. When I questioned them, they explained that they had studied together, so of course they'd missed the same questions. Going home that evening, I wished I had asked each girl to defend her test orally.

Dharma: The Lesson for Teachers

Since first penning this chapter, another incident in class compelled me to seize the Scantron forms of two young men who had been exchanging answers. Afterward, I felt sad rather than angry, and defeated rather than victorious. *Even though you got them?* a friend asked. Yes. Because when someone cheats, the tendency is to assume an object of the action: *Who got cheated?* As the instructor, it's easy to think they cheated *you* because they're getting away with something in your classroom behind your back. We feel sour and betrayed, and we certainly can't trust them. So, as advised by fellow profs and well-meaning veterans, we devise tricks to outfox them. At the very least, we stagger alternate versions of the test so that no one sits next to anyone else with the same version (something I neglected to do in this particular instance). We separate students, we surprise them, and some of us even stand on our desks.

The students, in their turn, invent new maneuvers. They create bathroom emergencies where they can access information hidden under their clothes, they clear their throats, they engrave key terms on their pencils and shoes, and they write in shorthand on their backpacks. They devise their own Morse code, with coughs and winks: one blink for True; two for False. They text each other. And in our turn, we prevent bathroom visits, we separate them from their buddies, and we watch. One colleague collects cell phones on test day, depositing them all into a cardboard box until all tests are turned in. And the go-round repeats itself year after year, in the coffee room as well as in the classroom, reliving itself in the confessions and exchanges between frustrated instructors.

It's a power struggle, with you as the teacher vying to maintaining control and authority. And like an invisible pollutant, it's the by-product of anxiety that arises with any unwanted but lingering conflict, fostering an equally unwanted punitive quality in the classroom. The silent tension is driven on by your belief that there is a price offenders must pay—for their own action and for its deterrent effect on the others watching.

But if we have the courage to point the wagging finger the other way, just as an experiment, it would allow us to ask if we're concluding falsely. Certainly cheating has reached epidemic proportions and needs to be regarded as such. But is it that they don't respect their teachers and the classroom, or anything else (especially honesty) as a basic virtue? Is it that they aren't interested in learning? Maybe it's not about any of that. But if it *is* respect they lack, we could ask ourselves where we failed to earn it, and if it's interest they lack, we might fashion new ways of awakening it.

Maybe they simply don't trust themselves. We might then ask ourselves how we can inspire that much-needed faith. Consider the tragedy: We don't trust them, and they don't trust themselves, either!

When Buddhism went from India to China, it fell into easy kinship with China's native Taoism. There is a Taoist phrase that resonates well with Zen's teaching regarding the trouble with pushing. It is known as *wu wei*, which is the "gentle way," and although it is translated from the Chinese as "non-doing," it doesn't always mean that we should actually do nothing. It's a reminder not to waste energy on pushing a stubborn agenda, one that is inevitably based on habits and fear. It means finding easier ways to live, and to solve conflicts, with less friction. This requires creativity, which is why renowned scholar and historian Huston Smith referred to *wu wei* as "creative quietude."

The heart of the matter is this: How can we make students choose *not* to cheat? For a student to choose not to cheat, she has to break out of the conditioned belief that getting ahead requires landing the grade at any cost, and it also means that we, as instructors, have to break out of the bonds of our own conditioned belief that students want to cheat and that they are against us. It means breaking old tactics that no longer serve us and dropping the suspicious mind-set. It means not allowing ourselves to lose our enthusiasm and warm regard for our students, because once that happens, we have set the conditions for burnout. Finally, it means breathing new life into the stale air of a tense classroom and opening up to inventive new ideas like those inspired by *wu wei*.

Create with the big I, Zen says.

Escaping from any conditioned trap requires a spirit of openness and the faith that doing things a different way will work. This quality of openness is thought of as "big mind" in Zen. With it comes the willingness to see beyond our own ego-driven desires and fears.

Ego-consciousness fosters the feeling of separateness, which makes us see ourselves as victims. From the perspective of the ego-mind, others are against us, out to defame us and one-up us, so we feel forced to fight for our due right to authority. We demand respect and we fight for control. When a driver refuses to let us in on the freeway, we take it as an assault; when a clerk refuses to honor our just-expired cards or coupons, we feel offended; when a student cheats, we feel our authority has been challenged.

As an experiment, consider the freeway example further. Imagine you need to be in the far-right lane in order to merge onto the other freeway. The line of cars in that lane is thick, and no one will let you in. You see one guy charge ahead even closer to the bumper in front of him just to prevent you from entering the lane.

Maybe you make the turnoff, maybe you don't. The bigger point has to do with your irritation and anger. I would pose the following question with regard to that one guy—we'll call him "the bully." If he had not been a bully, but had been instead a gentle-natured person, one incapable of refusing, would he have let you in? Most likely. But he was, for a multitude of uncountable reasons, not in the habit of extending himself toward others. He felt he needed to protect his space. So the situation could have gone one way or the other, depending on his—and this is key, *his*—tendency and frame of mind.

Looking at it this way, it's clear that his negligence had nothing to do with you. He didn't know you, didn't know your face or your name; he didn't register these things at all. It was all about him, not you! Imagine living with that hostility. Or it could be that he has a boss watching his every move and he's afraid to be late. It's a terrible position to be in. Whatever the case, he was undoubtedly suffering. Yet, out of our own paranoia, we take it as a move against us personally, and we try to pay the bully back—we give him a look, we yell, we try to speed ahead—all just to maintain our semblance of superiority and control.

Like the freeway bully, would you be willing to see the classroom cheater as a victim of her own fears? To be sure, we're not going to permit laziness or ignore a blatant lack of responsibility on the part of our students; we're enabling a shift in our own perspective and a corresponding shift in our approach to this problem. Would you be able to let go of what you thought you knew, of the methodology that hasn't worked so far, and leap into the nebulous, unknown world of trust, if you thought it could reveal creative new solutions to old challenges? If so, what solutions would you try?

Don't push the river, Zen says.

In Zen, the habit of *going against* is known as pushing the river. Allowing its flow requires abandoning the ego-mind—letting go of all its attachments and paranoia and venturing into new terrain where a multitude of possibilities might reveal themselves, depending on the situation and context. Zen tells us that the more we push, the more the world pushes back. In this case, it is an endless contest to gain an advantage over the other.

In the case of cheating, what would happen if students were encouraged to work together rather than against each other? If sharing answers was part of the game plan to begin with, then it might shift the mood from one of competition to one of cooperation, and we would be working with them rather than against them. They would be working together, helping each other succeed. Moreover, they would be able to celebrate one another's genuine progress and improved academic success, whether or not they currently realize that learning to work together makes for a better world.

We would stop pushing the river. We'd find a way to move with it. It would be *wu wei* in action. It would be a classroom where, as the kundalini yoga master Guru Singh has said in his weekly lectures, "no one passes until everyone passes."

"In this world there is nothing softer or thinner than water. But to compel the hard and unyielding, it has no equal. That the weak overcomes the strong, that the hard gives way to the gentle--this everyone knows, yet no one acts accordingly."

—Lao Tse, *Springs of Oriental Wisdom*

11

He Copied Me
The Zen Master Carries a Stick

I was seized by a feeling of déjà vu: *I've read this sentence before.* I launched a frenetic full-scale search through the already-marked-up papers in my lap. *I know I've seen all of this before,* I continued mumbling to myself after reading one student's paper. *It couldn't be my imagination,* I thought, as I did one double-take after another, stopping on certain paragraphs and hanging on certain phrases that rang out with unmistakable familiarity. I continued my frantic flipping through some seventy-five graded papers before finding it. *Aha!* It was identical. A word-for-word copy. The *Good job!* I had scrawled on top of the page in green ink, with a little happy face, yet, made me feel foolish. Of couse it was a good job—it was straight out of Wikipedia.

After passing back the papers, I asked the owners of the cloned papers to see me after class. I talked to each of them separately. The fact of copying was so shamelessly obvious that verifying it seemed almost redundant. I could hardly hold back a smirk when I pulled the first student aside and asked the perfunctory questions:

> Me: So, let's have it. Who copied whom?
> Allen: (Bewildered) What?
> Me: (More bewildered) What do you mean, *what?* Your papers!
> Allen: I really don't know. What's wrong?
> Me: (Incredulous) They're identical! Who copied whom?
> Allen: (More incredulous) What? I don't even know him!

My face must have spooked him into a guilty confession. After a few minutes of this go-round, he blamed his friend Michael for having copied him. He then softened the blame by further explaining that Michael's parents were very strict and that his friend would get kicked out of his house if he failed a course. Allen knew it was a mistake; he should have known better than to let his friend copy his paper, but he felt so sorry for him because it was his friend after all, and what could he do? Allen added that I should take pity on Michael as well.

I then talked to Michael, who said it was *Allen* who had done the copying. He explained to me that his friend Allen must have somehow gotten ahold of his paper and copied it without him knowing, but that I should be understanding because his friend suffers from depression and is under a lot of stress.

My impression after talking with both students was that neither of them could have written what they had turned in to me and that they must have copied their work from an external source.

When I discussed the situation with our department chairperson, I was hoping for an okay to simply drop them both from the class. She told me she always did just that in similar situations, but that new California rulings, which stipulated due recourse for students, forbade us from dropping them entirely for this infraction. I could only fail them on this one assignment.

And so, I advised the students to drop themselves, for several reasons: the obvious word-by-word plagiarism; the enormity of this crime; and further, the trouble it would save them in the long run should they force me to present their plagiarized work to the college disciplinarian. Just let it go, drop the course, and let it be a huge lesson, I advised. I received several e-mails from them during the interim between the incident and the day they dropped themselves from the class. This is one of them, unedited:

Dear Professor Quesada,
This is Allen from your Philosophy 22 class on Mondays and Wensdays. On Wensday when you returned the first essay that we wrote about hinduism you saw that my paper and my other friends were just alike, and you were RIGHT!, I will be honest with you this was my first class that im actually taking as enrolled as an SMC [Santa Monica College] student and i was really nervous of turning in the wrong work, or perhaps didnt want to get a bad grade. but what you did is right i am not arguing with you about that, but i was asking you, well begging you if you can please give us another chance please, i know what i did was wrong and i really did learn my lesson, you can also give us a 0 on this assigment and just let us continue on with our work and we both promise you that we'll do our own work and do good in your class. please Professor Quesada this is the first fall class and i just graduated from high school and i dont really want to have a bad name in this school, so please if you can find it in you to forgive us just this ONCE i would greatly and highly appreciate it. once agian thank you thank you

Dharma: The Lesson for Teachers

Even Zen masters use a stick sometimes.

I have spoken of the all-embracing nature of compassion and the spirit of forgiveness that it inspires when we learn to see through our habituated barriers. But compassion doesn't mean unqualified clemency. It doesn't mean anything goes, and it doesn't repeal the importance of accountability. Even Zen masters need to use a stick sometimes, and sometimes, even compassionate teachers may appear tough.

> *Just take care of what's in front of you,*
> Zen says.

How will you know when to simply watch and do nothing, and when to take resolute action?

The answer is, through your awareness—by being in tune with your surroundings. When my Zen teacher says, "You'll know what to do," I always used to wonder, How? How will I know? Because awareness brings insight. And opening to that state of awareness means letting go of stale ideas and trusting your instincts; because when everything else falls away—when the traces of the past and anxiety about the future fall away—there is only this present moment and our own honest response to it.

There has never been anything else but the present moment, yet we continue to reside in the fictional world of the past and the whimsical fantasies of the future. We miss the present, only to remember it later through the filter of our memory, which, far from infallible and limited by its perspective, magnifies and minimizes certain features of the story according to its fancy. And so it is that, strangely, we invent both the future and the past. The future has never existed, but when it unfolds into the present, we still continue on with our attention fixed on the time ahead, always living for the sake of this imaginary world that has taken on greater meaning than this one. We are a swinging pendulum jumping forward and backward—never stopping *here*. In this way, we live in a perpetual state of distraction, asleep to what is going on around us and, in effect, asleep for our very lives.

But *here* is where your intuition dwells. Here is where it comes to life and expresses itself with precision, eloquence, and conviction. Don't get stuck in your head, in the faux spheres of made-up time. Be here—it is all there is. Allow yourself to relax with the present and to be intimately acquainted with whatever is in front of you. Cherish the faith you have in yourself to handle it effectively, in the way you see fit at that present moment. Others' ways are not based on your situation; how could they be? Reality is always changing.

Subjective action comes from your sense of what's necessary and right, *right now*. Trust your discernment and respond to the situation, taking with you the proper amount of reservation as you choose among the barrage of theories thrown at you in pedagogy books—the ready-made methods that are based on data gathered in the past, or aimed at the future, or issued from someone else's experience. Your own presence of mind will lead to a direct and natural response, which isn't the same as a knee-jerk reaction and which certainly isn't the same as carelessness. Whereas a reaction comes from blindness, a direct response is guided by insight; and far from careless, *presence* means rising up to take absolute care of what's in front of you.

Lifeless, inflexible lesson plans and detached and static solutions that were designed to be universal in their application tend to feel stiff when held up to the rise and fall of actual circumstance. Grading is but one example, where percentages are calculated and grades are given without regard to individual and variable factors, such as the student's improvement over time and other relevant strengths the student may possess that outweigh the importance of numbers. There is also the consideration of "borderline" cases and how to deal with them fairly. Our dynamic attention to the host of multifarious circumstances that always present themselves unexpectedly thrives on our awakened instinct and experience. Resolving and coping with these circumstances with keenness and clarity is what sets us apart from computers. We have the power to make assessments through subjective estimation, by looking beyond the rows of check marks and by considering a wider array of virtues than numbers and outcome are able to show. Yet, because we live in a mathematical world that thrives on calculations and stakes its validity on theories and data, we have adopted the idea that there is no room for personal decision, and worse, we have become distrustful of our own intuition and inclinations.

Far from advocating rebelliousness or opposition—the very thing that diminishes inner peace and reinforces our imagined sense of separateness from the world—I am encouraging you to be true to yourself and to return to your own inherent intelligence, which reinstates inner peace and a sense of wholeness and connection with the world. It is the portal to a spiritual life.

Having faith in your intuition does not mean forever leaning on the soft side, being a bleeding heart, offering clemency to whoever asks. In the case of Allen and Michael, my intuition took stock of information I can scarcely enumerate. In a flash, it fused the images that would shape my course of action. In my mind's eye was a vivid montage: These two young students were in my class when I had previously turned away at least twenty others who had wanted to add the course. Those others would have jumped for the chance to occupy their seats and would have worked to keep them. They're young. Without vengefulness in my heart, I knew this would serve as an important lesson. I still feel, with a sense of consolation, that my having encouraged their own willful withdrawal was the dart that landed in the cherished middle spot—right between the overly lenient option of keeping them around as if everything was fine and the opposing alternative of sending them to the disciplinarian, where the event would have stained their college records forever.

12

I Expected More
from You
No Expectations

Joseph—I expected more from you. He wasn't looking at me, but my curt remark got his attention. After our eyes met, I went immediately back to topic and back to the class at large. He had been talking to his friend since before I started class, and either had no idea or simply disregarded the fact that class had started. I knew, as teachers always know, that their conversation had nothing to do with class. Their schoolboy laughter erupting at random when I hadn't said anything funny left no room for doubt.

That settled things for the moment. But because I was now scanning his general area at regular intervals, my attention was divided, and like a balloon with a fine leak, I could feel the intimacy drain from the class as a result. Yet I continued on with feigned enthusiasm.

It didn't take me long to learn that Joseph had a few years on his classmates, as we were becoming rapidly acquainted. My first encounter with this twenty-nine-year-old took place during the very first week of class by way of the same sort of chatter followed by the same sort of reprimand. That time, I split my request into two parts; namely, that he settle down and that he see me after class, thinking that I would nip the problem before it even had a chance to bud. During our conference that day, he explained that he was a returning student and that he already had a successful business selling cars. He was noticeably bright, and I told him so, but I also told him in an open spirit of honesty that I sensed he was fidgety. He admitted it was true, but promised to compose himself in class, and as part of our arrangement, he agreed to sit in the front of the class, away from his friend and all temptations.

Despite our pact, he had been coming in late and unabashedly helping himself to a seat in the back. It was a retrogression: Suddenly a seventh-grader again, he was sauntering off to the notorious back of the bus to blow spitballs with the other cool kids. Once, in the middle of our meditation, instead of waiting on the side until the end of the ten-minute silent period, like the other latecomers, he maneuvered his way through one of the crowded rows with a flashing phone to guide the way. His strobe-light cell phone was a hit, and every bit of attention it garnered widened his grin.

On another day—before we had the PA system installed—his buddy Alex raised his hand from the back row to tell me he couldn't hear me. He wanted me to speak louder. I wasn't new to lecturing in the large room, and I knew others could hear me fine. Rather than playing into his act, I simply suggested that he come to the front where he could hear me better. The logic was obvious, since he surely wouldn't have any trouble hearing me from just a few feet away, but the suggestion took him by surprise. He had no choice but to comply and drag himself up to the first row.

I expected more from Joseph because as an older student, he'd convinced me he wasn't there to waste his time. Nonetheless, at the end of the last day of the fourth week of the semester, his clock came to a sudden stop. His time in my class ran out.

On that day, Joseph and Alex were at it again. They were in one of the last rows of the back section, laughing and cavorting during my lecture. This time, with stony-faced seriousness and a you've-been-warned-too-many-times voice, I told them both to leave. No preamble, no comment, no explanation. Not even anger. Just the command. The next thing I knew, Joseph was on his way to the front of the class, walking toward the desk I was sitting on. Flustered, he yelled at me in front of everyone about the unfairness of it all, insisting that Alex was only passing him a piece of paper, even holding it up as evidence.

It was the first time in fourteen years that I'd had a student yell at me, but I didn't realize it immediately and was only surprised after the fact. The only thing I knew at that moment was not to feed the fire. I simply waited out the tirade and then calmly restated my request, and he left, slamming the door behind him. Trying to re-create a semblance of normalcy, I used the event as convenient foodstuff—however low in nutriment—for the lecture to follow.

I let it all digest as I ate my lunch that day, and then I e-mailed my chairperson for her recommendation on follow-up options. She answered reliably within minutes: *I wish I could tell you to drop him, but there's a protocol.* She included the links to the forms I would need to fill out and copied the e-mail to Ms. Bernstein, the campus disciplinarian, so that she could then watch for the forms. Although protocol prevented me from dropping him at once, I did have some recourse; according to my chairperson, I should suspend him for two class periods, or until he had been seen by Ms. Bernstein.

I filled out the forms and, in the space provided, compressed the relevant events into a matter-of-fact bulleted list, followed by my additional commentary and personal request that he be dropped:

- *This student has been verbally warned at least twice before to refrain from disrupting the class.*
- *He also signed the syllabus which warns against disruptions, and which states the possibility of being dropped because of such behavior.*
- *Upon the second verbal warning, he agreed, in a convincing tone, to discontinue sitting next to his friend and start anew.*
- *Despite our agreement, he continued sitting next to his friend. I let it slide so that he wouldn't say again that I was "singling him out."*
- *Today I had to ask them both to leave for the day, due to laughter and conversation between the two of them that continued while I lectured.*
- *This student, Joseph, threw up his arms in protest, and then made his way down to where I was standing and proceeded to yell at me in front of the entire class.*
- *While yelling in front of the class, he insisted he was only borrowing paper.*
- *Additional comments: Firstly, the disruptive conversation going on between them exceeded the simple act of a paper exchange. Secondly, this is a second-grade excuse. In the college classroom, they should come in prepared. Besides, yelling at me in front of the class with such aggression exceeds what is acceptable, and that is really the more important point now. I gave this student enough chances, and he took advantage of my kindness before finally going too far. Therefore, my preference in this case is that the student be dropped from my class.*

I followed up with Ms. Bernstein and made sure she knew Joseph would miss his test due to the suspension. Having only dealt with her once before on a different matter, I was unsure how long the process would take and whether or not Joseph would come to class on the day of the test.

He did. When I walked in, I saw him sitting next to Alex in the back as if nothing at all had happened. Unnoticed amid all the pre-test chatter, I motioned for them both to follow me outside. I addressed Joseph first in a simple, judicious tone that suggested the matter was not up for dispute: "Due to your inappropriate behavior last week, I cannot allow you to take the test, and you are not permitted to return until you meet with the campus disciplinarian." He argued. But as swiftly as you would snuff out a burning fire, I looked at him squarely and told him that a temper tantrum in class is never appropriate and then promptly turned to Alex. I handed him a warning, on an official form, and then told him he could return to his seat and take the test. Having heard my statement to Joseph, he asked, in a faint foreign accent, about the expression "temper tantrum." I told him what it meant and then told him he was allowed to take the test because he had not had one.

Joseph dropped. Alex continued on and never made trouble again, although I could tell he was unsure about where he stood with me.

After a few weeks, Alex came to ask me a question about Buddhism. But the question really wasn't about Buddhism; we had already finished that unit. He wanted to know if I had forgiven him. I answered his question just the same, and in a timeless moment, we regarded one another with the warmhearted air of forgiveness and with the silent promise of starting new.

In the weeks that had passed since "the incident," Alex had kept to himself, and I'd witnessed a great change in him. In that moment of kindliness, his smile told me he understood what didn't need to be said, and I smiled too. We both understood. He cared about my opinion of him, and I was profoundly happy about his transformation. That he had been listening, really listening, during these last few weeks had not escaped me. I had seen him sitting forward in his seat, I had felt his genuineness, and our eyes had met on those occasions. On this occasion, too, our eyes met. All that needed to be said was said. I told him wordlessly that I'd noticed his earnest commitment to the class. He was forgiven. Just like that.

Dharma: The Lesson for Teachers

Joseph's story unfolded as it did regardless of any expectations I had. But situations like this one are reminders to stay in touch with your own motivation when presented with a problem student. Make sure your interest is pure and that your only desire is appropriate resolve rather than *winning*. Don't indulge the fantasy that you are a victim. A person who yells is an angry person, and an angry person is a suffering person. So, too, a student who yells is an angry student who, whether rightly or wrongly, feels victimized. More victims in the world means more needless suffering. Act swiftly and then let it go. Remember, the behavior had little to do with you personally.

We are all on different points along our individual paths. When confronted with a student whose purpose, it seems, is to bring you grief, consider the importance of your role in bringing him to the next step along his respective journey. Even a short-lived case like Joseph's is undoubtedly packed with lessons that will come to fruition in the future and, thus, are impossible to imagine now.

Each situation is a blossom to be picked with a curious spirit. It is believed in Tibetan Buddhism that each situation we encounter, pleasant or unpleasant, is exactly what we need at the time. It teaches us to confront our mind-state and all the unchecked reactions that pop up like springs out of past conditioning. It teaches us to direct our energy into response rather than reaction. It teaches us to be present as every situation is new. Because it is new, there is no surefire formula. What you do comes out of your conscious response, and what you take from it comes from your curiosity.

Have no expectations, Zen says.

Having no expectations leaves nothing else but to work with the situation *as it is,* rather than as you think it should be. And then you move on.

Enter into the sound of no-sound, Zen says.

Alex flourished when left to the solitude of his own person. He flourished, or he simply came back to his true self—what Zen would call his *ordinary self,* untainted by the distraction and negative persuasion of others. He came into his own stillness.

Entering into your own stillness allows you to discover a boundless field, a tranquility and a vastness that wasn't apparent before, because the noise we are so accustomed to crowds it out. Just as we're habituated to continuous action, we're similarly habituated to continuous chatter. We're compelled to fill every gap with words, which we consider to be the only valid source of communication. We're told that to exist is to *do,* to live is to *accomplish,* to resolve is to *solve,* and to interact is to *say,* with our expressions following suit, such as that normal break in conversation we have come to call the "awkward silence."

When you learn to completely immerse yourself in experience, you suddenly see that discussion of that experience becomes immaterial. The endless chatter just falls away. It is seen as secondary, as debris in the crystal-clear waters. It suddenly becomes insignificant and fails to do the experience justice. Discourse has its rightful place and purpose, just as every good tool does, but often the most significant moments in our lives exceed the potency of these tools. For example, the description of love can't relay the divine experience of love, nor can the explanation for floating convey the feeling of weightlessness in the water. Describing these moments with words sometimes feels as absurd as using a wrench on the sky to stop the rain.

Experience the experience.
—Guru Singh

One of my spiritual teachers always reminds us in his public talks to *experience the experience* because strangely, we need cajoling to do what seems inevitable. He knows it requires courage to enter into the silence that all spiritual traditions speak of. It requires courage to fall into that space where we are no longer clouded by the noise of our own thoughts and by our need to prove anything. It requires courage to let go of the only way we have ever been taught to do things. It requires courage to simply be here, and to trust that, often, that is enough. I couldn't save Joseph's place in the class, but I could start anew with Alex. It requires courage to listen and be present in order to hear—to be present in order to be open so that at last, in that openness, we can discover what words couldn't express.

"We think there is something to attain, something outside of ourselves, but everything is already here."

—Thich Nhat Hahn, *The Pocket Thich Nhat Hanh*

13

Police Prof
The Borrowed Badge of Brawny Might

After a sequence of certain events, I metamorphosed into a warden that semester. The first of these events was an ongoing dialogue I had been having with my colleague Rose, who teaches yoga and dance at a nearby university. It must have been something in the air that semester, because we both had parallel stories to share about miscreants and misadventures.

She was outraged that even in her yoga class, where it might be reasonable to expect a tranquil mood, the general decorum was anything but peaceful and was even lacking in basic manners. Cell phones routinely go off, she explained, and with each routine tardy, rather than gingerly entering in the back of the room so as not to draw attention to themselves, they walk in front of the room, knocking over water bottles and stepping on other people's mats in order to roll out their own.

I had just listened to the crowning point of Rose's travails over coffee one morning when I encountered the second event, in the form of economics professor Mel. Entering my own class a few minutes early, I cornered the notoriously hard-hitting instructor before she left the room:

Me: Does it seem like there's more talking and fooling around this semester than before?

Mel: Oh, I've got zero tolerance for that crap. They're out the door if they pull that, and they're dropped that same day. It's right there in the code of conduct—you disrupt others, that's grounds for dismissal. We have to consider the group over the individual.

Her no-nonsense credo hit me like a stimulant—a swig of bitter espresso that fired an irritating but addictive charge through my whole body. While setting up for class, the buzz continued, and with a new sense of irony, I inserted my DVD for the day into the player: peace advocate and Buddhist monk Thich Nhat Hanh on the subject of anger. Infused with an intoxicating sense of power and resolve, I policed the room while they watched the video, sniffing out nefarious pockets of whispering and hidden emissions of any sort, which I detected in smatterings—three girls gossiping here, two others texting over there, and muffled laughter in the back. Always in the back, and nowhere to be found when I looked closer.

I finally caught some offenders in the act: two girls chatting instead of watching the film. I asked them to follow me outside where I scolded them for their behavior. "I see you're having trouble concentrating today," I said. "Why don't you take the day off and get it out of your system, and then come back on Thursday when you're ready to be in class." But before I let them go, I squeezed a little more air out of the bellows: "I find it disappointing that at this level I should have to reprimand you for not being able to sit quietly in class."

After the film ended, three other girls (whose names I now know well) started whispering as I began our discussion. The following semester, I would be in a different room with a different group, and in a different state of mind; to a similar provocation, I would ask the offenders out loud, with a bit of crooked humor, if they would like to stop fooling around or if they would prefer that I go to the dark side. The *Star Wars* reference would get a chuckle all around, and the talkers would stop their disturbance with good feelings. This time, however, after moving the girl in the middle to the front of the room, I administered a grand and dramatic speech, in a solemn tone, with the microphone on:

"I had to excuse two people today, and now I'm moving another. It's incredible to me that at the college level, I have to do this—I have to be a spy and a disciplinarian. I'd much rather talk about the exalted topics of our course, about the wandering holy men of India and the ancient wisdom of China. But, I say to myself, 'Maybe they don't know any better; after all, it is the fall semester. Maybe they've just come from high school; maybe they're new to the world, and they don't know that they have to comport themselves a certain way in the college classroom, that they're being rude if they talk while the instructor is talking. They don't know that they're being disruptive to the serious students. But if they *do* know better, then there's only one conclusion to be drawn: They're being selfish, not caring one bit that they're bothering the many other serious students that truly want to learn.'"

After a pause, I threw in the bit from Mel: "That's why it's right there in SMC's Code of Conduct: If you disrupt others, you will be dropped from class, so this is going to stop now." (Addressing the three girls) "You three who had to be reprimanded today, you're going to write me a three-page essay explaining why you were disrupting the class, and you're going to e-mail it to me by Friday. You're going to explain in your essay the ways in which your behavior was selfish, and I don't care if you have to study for other tests in other classes or if you have a pile of work to do for other instructors—your paper will be done, and I will have it by Friday."

After class the three of them came to my desk. One was apologetic, one was resentful, and one was businesslike. They each turned their papers in to me on time and demonstrated a marked improvement in their behavior. At the time, although I knew all too well that dropping students was not as easy as Mel made it out to be, I felt vindicated by my speech, as if I had affirmed my own sense of self-respect and, especially, my sense of control in the classroom.

Dharma: The Lesson for Teachers

What we do flows naturally from our state of mind, which is either tuned in or scattered. And when it's scattered, we go flying off all too easily on the whims of paranoia and suspicion, where ego, guided by its need for power and assurance, leads the way. I had a unique combination of ingredients that semester: my own burnout, a double-sized class, and the chance occurrence of many students having arrived in packs. That is to say, I had a group that was composed of many mini groups, which I determined to be long-established high school cliques, little sisterhoods and fraternities whose loyalties superseded the latent will of its individual members. The resultant raucous atmosphere, itself the fallout of the requisite joining-in that is part of any clique's duties, contributed to the disjunct among us and to the general disarray. The sense of connection I like to create in the class was palpably absent; I knew in my heart that any tactic I employed would only reinforce the comfortless environment of the room and wouldn't really fix things. I knew it was more about *being* than *doing*.

Ego is a blindfolded driver that steers us into our woes. From the Eastern point of view, ego is always the source of our troubles. It is sometimes subtle and sometimes shamelessly bold; although we often don't recognize it in ourselves, it's everywhere. It's the obnoxious uncle that talks too loudly at parties; it's the screaming diva who wants it now, the competitive coworker, the insecure bully looking for reassurance, the suspicious husband, the oversensitive mother, the tyrant, the control freak, and the worrywart. It's all of us. And it's the source of all our fears.

It's the fire under the vile brew that drives us into a desperate need to assert our control, which, in the absence of a true sense of connection, is displayed as sarcasm, as myriad, inorganic attempts at action, rendered futile by not being rooted in the heart.

We can't change anything effectively until we realize the dependence that exists between our own state of mind and the rest of the world. This is one of Buddha's pivotal teachings, and the one that is most counterintuitive to the Western mind, which is conditioned by a tendency to see the world in dualistic terms, with us standing apart and separate from it. The inevitable effect is that we see ourselves in an oppositional stance, forced to defend ourselves against everyone, constantly regarding others with suspicion.

It is the ego-led self-consciousness that creates this sense of separation between ourselves and everything else, deceiving us into a disjointed view of the world. And through our obstructed lens, the world is flanked into opposing categories that appear just as solid and sure as man standing separate from woman, black from white, and east from west. But, as the dew lifts from the glass, we see what was previously hidden. As our lens changes, what we see also changes.

Such polarities are seen with time as shades on a spectrum rather than as stark opposites. They are mutually dependent parts of a whole. Where humans and nature were once seen as disconnected rivals in conflict, we have as a culture recently come to recognize our inseparability from the environment that nurtures us and our complete dependence on it. It is an inviolable bond. The division between interior and exterior, or "me" and "not me," breaks down when we consider that we depend as much on our own vital organs as we do on oxygen and all the oxygen-giving vegetation that sustains them. The ability to see our place in nature differently had to take place before we could start to affect positive changes in the environment as a whole. A shift in perspective always alters the tenor of any situation; the sound of a siren in the middle of the night can be a source of annoyance, but with a change of viewpoint, it is also the sound of a life being saved. Either way, it is the same siren; only the listener's perspective has changed.

There is an unbreakable connection between what is seen and the eyes that see, between what is heard and the ears that hear. Your perspective shapes your interpretations, and in this way, you create your world. To see this is to overcome duality and to enter into unity. As an experiment, ask yourself what shift within your own way of seeing would bring about the desired shift in the atmosphere of your classroom.

A change in perspective requires that you at once drop your attachments to the agendas and templates laid down by others. Thus, a change in perspective engenders an inevitable liberation. But you have to have faith in yourself and jump. This faith is what dislodges all the doubts and second-guessing connected with the issue of control.

Second-guessing yourself is mental clutter. That's not to say you should be reckless. It simply means that you need to sweep out the cobwebs of comparison in order to return to the state known as *naturalness* in Zen. Letting go of the residue that comparisons entail enables uncluttered freedom of action, which is not only free, but inherently and instinctively right, because it is in tune, in context, and done in presence of mind. Comparing your actions with others puts you in immediate conflict with your surroundings and results in frustration and self-consciousness, with you wrangling with your own mess of muddled thoughts. *Mel wouldn't tolerate this whispering. I shouldn't either. They're getting away with it.*

> *When you have something in your consciousness you do not have perfect composure,* Zen says.[2]

Cleaning out the mental clutter is at the very heart of what is known as *practice* in Zen. And cleaning out the clutter is to drop

---

2. Shunryu Suzuki, *Zen Mind, Beginner's Mind.* Boston: Shambhala Publications, Inc., 2011.

the source of it all—the ego-mind, with its self-consciousness, fears, and doubts. It is why monks meditate for hours facing a wall and why laypeople support them. It's why millions of modern Asians still maintain the near-sacrosanct tradition of the ego-effacing bow. And it's why their artists unveil for us the spirit of the ephemeral in their work; perceiving the vanity of flattened-out perfection, they eschew the symmetrical in favor of the imperfection that is life itself, in all its raw splendor and changeableness. Built into the fabric of their being is the imperative to symbolically refuse vanity, and to wholly lay down the ego—a function that is at the very heart of what it means to be human.

The ego is the source of mental clutter. It's that old clunker that never stops spewing out its toxic gunk, propelling clouds of poisonous debris into the sky and into the world. All the anger, greed, and ignorance—known as the Three Poisons in Buddhism—start with the ego, and as long as it's there, it keeps us trapped in our own detached frame of mind, stuck in our heads, and enclosed within our own world of self-consciousness, where natural action is impossible.

To be natural is to be sincere. Without sincerity, life is a battleground. I never forgot the simple aphorism repeated often by one of my spiritual teachers: To pursue the spiritual life, one needs both sincerity and awareness. The spiritual life is, at heart, only a search for these two simple but elusive qualities.

The fear and suspicion create a gap between us that makes sincere action impossible, because behind that wall of separation and self-consciousness, we have convinced ourselves that we could control our world by opposing it. As if we could escape a riptide by swimming against it! In our dualistic mind-set, we believe we can fix our surroundings by opposing them. But as we begin to chisel away at that wall, we find we can more easily express ourselves in our own way and that we can restore the harmony in our environment more fluently in a spirit of naturalness with no antagonism.

He who relies on force does not conquer,
Taoism says.

What folly it would be, mused the old Chinese sage Chuang Tzu, to try to shorten a crane's legs to make it more like a duck while trying to lengthen a duck's legs so that it may be more like a crane! Mel's way was right for Mel. Was I a crane walking like a duck? The simple act of asking the question is the beginning of "turning the arrow inward," rather than pointing it continually outward for the source of the problem.

Sometimes we just see things wrong, or we're overly sensitive. While writing this book, I attended a small memorial for a Jewish relative. Because I was tuned into it, I watched as my ninety-year-old grandmother leaned over and indulged in a whispered conversation with the woman next to her while the rabbi was talking. I watched as he continued to talk, apparently unbothered by this, even though we were a small group clustered together and their whispering was completely obvious. He seemed to think it was normal.

In the context of the classroom, this kind of behavior is arguably out of place and disrespectful. But when it happens, seize those moments as opportunities to skillfully redirect your energy.

Next time you are vexed, examine your own mind-set and motivation and ask yourself if your behavior is sincere. "Control" then becomes a matter of being in harmony. It is a tuned-in response. It may be a more humorous response, it may be a gentler response, or you may come to see it as a nonissue. Your response is yours alone, and it is totally uncontrived and in sync, just as a good drummer responds to a quick change in the guitarist's rhythm, dwelling in the zone musicians call "the pocket," where they're in step and intertwined. And in that placeless space comes that unnamable feeling that issues from true coherence with others without a trace of any barrier, resistance, or hesitation.

"*Built into the very structure of the ego self is a need to oppose, resist, and exclude to maintain the sense of separateness on which its continued survival depends. So there is 'me' against the 'other,' 'us' against 'them.'*"

—Eckhart Tolle, *Stillness Speaks*

14

Inching Backward
Who's Out of Tune?

Almost two months after the semester was over, I received an e-mail from a student named Moshe:

Dearest Professor:
I hope you are enjoying your holiday vacation. I really miss your class. I got a B. I was wondering what I can do to raise my grade from a B to an A. I'm ready to do anything—I need it to get into UCLA. Please.

This type of e-mail was nothing new, but this was a student that I considered lucky to get a B, and it was long after the usual wave of similar end-of-semester pleas that flood my inbox.

I remembered him. He had the kind of face that seemed to be sculpted into a permanent expression of jest. One day, early on in the semester, I had to move Moshe to the front of the class, along with two others.

He had been either joking around right then, or else had just finished joking around and still couldn't shake the laughter off his face. I could tell he was easily distracted by anything. I told him this would be his new seat for the semester. Sometimes students seem thankful when I move them, grateful for being physically placed in a situation, away from temptation, where they can become serious students. But Moshe seemed to think the whole affair was silly and unnecessary.

Me: It'll be good for you, you'll see.
Moshe: I don't know why you think I'm fooling around. I don't know what I'm doing wrong. I just want to do good.
Me: Then this is perfect. Good students sit in the front. It'll keep you out of trouble and away from temptation.

He laughed and shook his head at the folly of it all.
The very next day, he was two rows farther back, next to his friend. Every time I glanced his way, he would look up at me in full attention, with serious eyes, and exaggerated interest. The day after, he was farther back still, and on that day, I addressed him.

Me: I thought you were going to sit in the front.
Moshe: (With a surprised expression) Oh, did you want me to go to the front?
Me: Yes, I would like you to go to the front.

Although he moved to the front on that occasion, Moshe contributed to my edginess that semester, keeping me distracted with the feeling that the minute I looked away, he would start with his clowning. But the e-mail request that came long after semester's end suggested that either he was playing dumb or that he had been clueless about the extent his behavior had bothered me and, more importantly, that it hadn't been purposeful.

Dharma: The Lesson for Teachers

Buddha spoke of the Three Poisons—greed, anger, and ignorance—the roots of all suffering and dysfunction. The most compelling part about them is that they start inside us, as seeds which are dispersed like pollen through our thoughts, words, and actions. Compassion and wisdom are the antidotes. Nurturing these qualities requires the courage to ask ourselves (and even more courage to then admit) when we've been acting from motives tainted by these toxic seeds.

When I think back to the semester with Moshe, I realize that I never even had a true heart-to-heart with him. He came to my desk after class one day when I was already surrounded by at least ten other students, each of whom had their own various problems and questions. With a few words and an assurance from him that it wouldn't happen again, he was on his way. Even near the front of the room, he did continue to disrupt the class occasionally, but I wonder to what extent a true connection or a different tactic would have produced a different outcome. The problem is that our irritation holds us back. We're peeved, and in the midst of an ego trip, we get caught up in showing the other who's boss.

I proceeded in a climate of annoyance, awash in an air of suspicion. I entered the room that semester and delivered my lectures with no sense of connection. That disconnect is the outgrowth of ignorance, known in Zen as the worst of the three poisons, because unlike the usual way we think of the word, as a deficiency of information, *ignorance* in the Buddhist sense refers to the blindness between us, which in turn breeds fear. Especially the fear of losing control. The result is an internal hellfire kept alive by the perpetual distrust of others' motives. Most unsuccessful discipline is guided by this fear—with the assumption that the "other" is against us—and this is no less true inside the classroom, where we feel our power is under siege. So readily kicking out offenders makes us feel like they didn't win—we did. But what a shame! They'll have missed out on the class, and we'll have missed out on an opportunity to reach a student. So, even though it would have been easier to kick Moshe out—always the easier solution—I would not have won. I would have failed.

The twin pillars of wisdom and compassion allow us to chip away at that perceived wall of separation. With that wall gone, we are no longer prisoners of our own making, and with that wall gone, the cool breeze of equanimity may take its place. We look around and everything is *fine*, and we feel light, and we smile, and even when things are not completely fine, we still feel absolutely *capable*.

Wisdom overcomes ignorance. And in this balanced mental state, there is nothing left to prevent compassion. One way to enter into this state is to simply recognize the inevitability of change. The fact of impermanence and its relationship with compassion isn't obvious at first, but consider the simple example of mistaken first impressions. We often have the wrong idea of people at first, thinking them unfriendly before later realizing our mistake.

As an experiment, try to remember a situation in which one of your good students inexplicably changed and fell horribly behind in class. And conversely, consider a time when one of the unruly students—someone you had decided was a troublemaker—suddenly turned herself around. Has it ever happened that the worst of your students later became a favorite? Remembering this allows us to let go of the attachments we have to our ideas and expectations and generates the state of mind—known in the Tibetan tradition as *Bodhicitta,* or "enlightened heart"—whose natural state of equanimity keeps us neutral in our treatment toward others. *To see* change is at the same time *to allow* change. It is to let go of your resistance to it and to welcome the inevitable changes to come in others. To see into the process of this world in flux is to see the world *becoming* and to relax with it. And then, even if the entire semester is doomed, it is to see into that, too—to see that it will soon unfold into an entirely new one, and with it, a new opportunity to make the next one better. It is to let go. It is to embody the equanimous mind and the compassionate heart that is at once patient and accepting.

The heart-to-heart I could have had with Moshe took place later with another student. I went back to the offender's seat, put my hand on his shoulder, and without rancor, told him I wanted us to speak after class. He responded to my sincerity. Our meeting was short, but direct and honest. And he never repeated the offense. I explained this time why it was important to me that students refrain from carrying on their own private conversations in class, telling him that it distracts others and makes it stressful on me to have to yell over their voices. I also said that it makes me feel like

I'm wasting my time, enthusiasm, and effort. I further explained that in a large class, it takes even more work to create a sense of connection and then concluded with my forthright request for his cooperation, to which he agreed. We parted with positive feelings.

You transform the universe you inhabit,
Zen says.

When others witness the equanimous mind, they witness something that is intuitively correct. There is power in truth. When you act with wisdom and compassion, which are reflected in your open spirit, your students witness a loving way to respond to provocation—a preferable and positive alternative to the anger they see every day all around them, on the roads, in their homes, on the television, and among their friends. They are more likely to do as they see rather than as they're told. We see small examples of this kind of contagiousness every day, such as when we meet someone whose spirit is so jubilant that we find ourselves mimicking their enthusiasm, smiling bigger, and imbibing their glee. And conversely, we sometimes allow ourselves to be brought down by those whose energy is lethargic. The power we all have to transform our universe is infinite, and it all starts with our state of mind.

To look inward, to consider our own state of equanimity first before addressing others, is reflected in a charming story one of my spiritual teachers told us one night while affixing the capo to his guitar: "Last week, I kept wondering why Scott was playing an odd chord, so I looked back at him a few times, but then I thought, 'Well, he knows more about chords than I do—maybe there's a reason,' and it stopped being odd. But after class, Scott asked me if there was a reason I was playing in a lower key." It was him all along.[3]

Always ask, *Am I the one out of tune?*

---

3. Guru Singh, lecture, Los Angeles, September 15, 2009.

15

From a Bellow to a Whisper
Do the Opposite

Returning tests can quickly turn into an ordeal; a deceptively simple operation that has the potential to bust apart at the seams, a test of patience, a routine classroom chore that converts itself on a dime into a humongous hassle. As long as anyone knows anyone else in the class, they'll share results: *What did you get? What was the answer to number four? Yes! No! Oh, my GOD!* Which, in a small group, is fine because the moderate size of the class serves as built-in damage control. But in a large one—one sectioned into tightly bound coalitions since high school—the excited whispers grow from a light drone to a cacophony of either distressed squeals or shouts of joy in seconds.

It was a clear and bright October morning when I stepped into the windowless lecture hall with the bundle of graded tests under my arm. As I approached, one anxious student flagged me down to ask if I would be returning their exams. (The following year, I would make the decision to hold them until after my lecture, but on this day, my answer was "Yes, I will return them in a moment.")

As I began to call out the names penciled onto the answer sheets of their first exam, the noise started almost immediately. My sympathies went to the ones who anxiously strained to catch an echo of their own name. I recalled, at that moment, the carnival game where you squirt water into the clown's mouth to make the balloon expand. As I darted up and down the side steps of the tiered hall to facilitate speedy delivery, I had devious thoughts: *Perhaps I should have figured out a way to put the talkers' names on the bottom of the stack.* I knew, roughly, who they were. The distorted balloon was set to pop against the needle. I didn't have a PA system then, so I threw my voice into the cacophonous roar, yelling their names in order to be heard. I shushed them, and the ones who were still listening shushed the people around them. "If you guys want your tests back, you need to be quiet."

On the day of the next go-round, while getting ready to return their second exams, I went to task like a commando officer, watchful and waiting to ambush. I didn't want a repeat of the first run. But this time, as the inevitable clamor mushroomed, I intuitively got softer, calling names so they could barely be heard. As always, the ones who hadn't yet received their tests silenced themselves immediately and yelled at the others to do the same. But once they had their tests in hand, the motivation to stop comparing notes with their friends across the aisle disappeared, and the raucousness spread across the room like a swarm of behemoth bees with bullhorns.

So I simply stopped. And then they stopped. Mission aborted. *You can get your tests after class,* I announced without any further ado. Amid a chorus of disappointed moans, I made a swift U-turn, calmly walked back to my desk, opened my notebook, and started a soft introduction to our next topic.

On subsequent occasions, I found that I merely had to soften my voice to avoid this kind of drama.

Dharma: The Lesson for Teachers

As in the domain of parenting, there is much arguing about methodology in discipline. Likewise in teaching. There is no incontestable formula that all teachers agree on, and no universally accepted, surefire rule that will work every time, by every teacher, in every situation. But if there were, it would be the one about following through. Mean what you say and follow through—especially at the beginning of the year when you're introducing yourself and setting the tone for the rest of the semester.

My repeated requests for quiet, through repeated remonstrations, both subtle and explicit, left no room for ambiguity. Although I hadn't expressly said I would stop if they didn't stop, I knew intuitively that without a decisive consequence to their continued chatter, all directives from that point on would lose all meaning.

In an ideal world, we wouldn't have to play the discipline game at all, especially at the college level. But, when discipline is necessary, try a swift but gentle correction, one whose surprising quietude prompts change more powerfully and effectively than the loud and blatantly punitive measures we're all used to and which only tend to add to the noise and agitation.

I hadn't planned on pulling what I now call, with a bit of humor, a "stop and switch," but it was born out of the need to avoid contributing to the clamor. I wanted to make a strong point in a soft way. As an experiment, try your own version of *doing the opposite* the next time you find yourself about to fall into the old patterns of reprimanding at the expense of your own energy and inner peace. For example, instead of hollering out all the usual verbal commands in the face of continued opposition, try watching them without saying a word and continue watching for a good swollen moment and see what happens.

Doing the opposite has to be deliberate; think of it as *purposeful reticence*. It reverses your habitual impulses. It marks new tracks and reconditions locked-in tendencies that don't serve a purpose anymore. As an analogy, consider a swimmer who reconditions bad habits only by nurturing new ones by doing laps with better form or with more efficient movements, for example. By practicing purposefully, the corrected form gets imprinted into the brain and into the muscles as muscle memory, leaving the swimmer with more energy, more efficient motion, and less exhaustion. Perhaps the original reflex was to kick harder to gain speed, but with conscious effort, the swimmer learns that all that extra kicking only depletes her energy and does little to advance her race.

Similarly, a sailor out at sea knows better than to sail against the wind. And it is the same principle of gentle action, *wu wei,* which guides the martial artist in disciplines like judo and kung fu. Conserving his energy, the judo master economizes his movement; like an efficient machine, he maximizes his output while minimizing his input. He uses surprise and subtlety rather than opposition, and clever sidesteps rather than brute force. He redirects his opponent's energy rather than exhausting his own. He demonstrates the way of nonresistance, which cautions against the folly of direct opposition. As subtle and elegant as these actions are, they're also wholly deliberate.

Doing the opposite conserves energy by taking the gentler approach. In the classroom, it might be as simple as not buying into the frustration that arises in the face of misbehavior. Cherish your calm center above anything else, and find your refuge there rather than getting caught up in the whirlwind. Pull yourself out of the storm as a surfer would skillfully pull out of a riptide—not by paddling against the current.

The same idea, found in old yogic wisdom, advises that we put our energy into reaffirming what we *do* want rather than contributing to what we *don't* want. The kundalini yoga master Guru Singh once spoke of the need to "appreciate the difference." He was urging us to *create* rather than to complain, to gently *construct* rather than destroy. Repairing a broken situation is often easier than we think. By merely emphasizing the desired behavior, as opposed to condemning the undesired behavior, we bring it to fruition. "Want something to be different? Then appreciate the difference," he said.[4] And in the classroom, if you don't like noise, then appreciate silence.

This takes courage. And although it's not obvious at first, I came to see why. It is because, strange as it seems, we are addicted to the dismal. As the mystic Andrew Harvey once noted, our curious fear of freedom and joy tends to show up as we proceed along our spiritual journeys.[5] The mind, like all things in nature, is bound by the law of inertia and rolls along like a heavy truck in its own

4. Guru Singh, lecture, Los Angeles, November 26, 2009.

5. Andrew Harvey and Mark Matouske, *Dialogues with a Modern Mystic.* Wheaton, IL: Quest Books, 1994.

laziness, suspicious of change and difference. It'll linger in familiar dark places until we willfully and purposefully shift into overdrive and pull ourselves out of it with courage and curiosity.

Become aware of when you start to feel annoyed. That awareness is the watch light that allows you to catch yourself before snapping like a rubber band and to replace that reflex with purposeful action. It's not suppression; it's reconditioning. It's fully conscious, willful action. Even a subtle but decisively taken "nonaction" is a powerful one because, done willfully, it's no longer an enslaved action. It is to act without acting.

Annoyance can quickly escalate into anger, but awareness lets us catch it before it does. Although it used to be more common for therapists to instruct their patients to "get it all out" when struggling with emotions like anger, the logic is starting to change. It is now more widely understood that this kind of behavior only feeds the habit energy.

A friend recently brought my attention to a reality show called *Celebrity Detox*. I watched as patients were taken to a junkyard and then told to smash things with baseball bats. As the Vietnamese monk and peace activist Thich Nhat Hanh has explained in his writings, by engaging in violent behavior, you are just "rehearsing it" and reaffirming it rather than curtailing it. By venting, you are nurturing the combustible mixture of blame and resentment, clinging to the short-lived illusion of relief due only to the effect of exhaustion. How much better to nourish true insight, to invite the gift of tranquility that is rooted in true awareness, and to step into a true refuge that will forever serve you.

With large classes a consistent part of my teaching load, I am equally consistent in returning tests at the end of class, along with the (emphatic) reminder that they're free to leave as soon as they've received their own. It has proven itself to be a better method. Of course, in a big class, merely taking roll can quickly slip into mayhem, but when it starts, I stop.

16

The iPod Guy
Everything Happens at the Right Time

In a bit of irony, I happened to see the slightly peculiar movie *A Serious Man* while writing this chapter. The Coen Brothers movie, set in the 1960s, introduces us to a rambunctious adolescent named Danny Gopnik who is sitting in Hebrew class, not learning Hebrew. Instead, he is blasting his ears out with earphones, what was then an unknown modern piece of technology. When the tired old teacher yanks at the wires, the miniature speakers come unplugged and the sound of Jefferson Airplane floods the room.

I had a Danny Gopnik in my class, too. It was early in the morning, and the tall rebellious kid sat slumped in his seat, hiding under his black hoodie. Eyes closed, his head was bobbing to the music that was blasting through his iPod at such a high volume, everyone could hear the alternating booms and muffled treble—except me. The minute I paused, however, the tinny resonance reached my ears. As I looked around to trace its source, I found the class already watching me with the we-have-been-waiting-for-you-to-notice look. When I witnessed his nonchalance, my face came unzipped, and with all my features now hanging open in astonishment, I simply pointed to the door. He knew, and didn't resist or say a thing.

"Why bother coming to class?" I asked. No one attempted to answer my rhetorical question, and iPod guy never returned to answer it either.

In another bit of irony connected with this anecdote, it turned out to be a ready example of the day's teachings. I had prepared to talk about Confucius's philosophy of propriety that day, which centers on the social graces that were of primary importance to the Chinese philosopher. The teachings are about decorum and manners and include the kinds of concerns Western philosophers have generally brushed aside as irrelevant froufrou. Still today, it is looked upon by philosophers as the stuff of etiquette—the stuff of Emily Post, or maybe Martha Stewart, but definitely not serious philosophy. However, for Confucius, exemplifying the niceties that compose good social form was where it all started. That kind of personal refinement was, for the wise old teacher, the foundation of a civilized society as a whole. It was considered to be the distinguishing mark of an educated human being, the finishing touch, the gilded trim on a fine silk brocade.

Dharma: The Lesson for Teachers

Take advantage of these synchronic events, even when one of them is not the sort you would have invited. They never are; the very nature of disturbances is that they come by surprise. Be awake and ready to harvest even the weeds. Don't get swept up for too long in the offense.

Certainly this boy was not Confucius's model of a proper young man. He wasn't respectful of the classroom environment or of me, his teacher, and he was wasting his own time. Confucius was a traditionalist; he defined the expression "standing on ceremony." He also had a punchy side and probably would have given the kid a good whack with his cane.

But the inflexibility of Confucius and his teachings has been balanced from the beginning, in China, by the Taoist delight in spontaneity. When I was a student, I remember hearing that the reflective Chinese is Confucian on the outside and Taoist on the inside. The opposite forces stabilize one another, like those birch trees with multiple trunks, where one of them, driven by some wayward impulse, leans stubbornly to one side, ready to fall, but never does. Its very lassitude anchors the others, giving poise to the whole entity. Likewise, the mysticism of the Tao, and later, of Buddhism, complemented the patriarchal rigidity of Confucianism in China, where neither one was predominant.

Buddhism was the newcomer—China's adopted Indian child—that quickly recognized its kinship with the native Taoist mysticism and that led to a commingling that gave shape to Zen (*Ch'an* in Chinese) and to a penchant for looking at life's inherent humor, represented by the lovable, big-bellied, laughing Buddha. Just as Zen balances the formalism of Confucian teachings, we can find our own footing between extremes by maintaining order and issuing the necessary directives, but without losing our way back to the lighthearted center. In so doing, we transform life's stinking weeds into fragrant blossoms.

On one level we can and do make a distinction between weeds and flowers, but yet, on another, we can still continue to see everything as absolutely perfect, where the weeds are exactly as they should be and where everything occurs at just the right time.

Weeds always pop up out of nowhere. No holes were dug and no seeds were sown. They just appear, and when they do, you pull them out. My student, iPod guy, sat in his wooden school desk just like all the other nineteen-year-olds in the class, until one day near the end of the term, he popped. We were all set to define Confucius's ideal gentleman—the one with perfect comportment and elegant, proper manners. And on that day, the flattened spring came uncoiled. As if on cue, as if it had been part of some quirky scenario in a play, he prompted me to demonstrate the proper by pointing to the improper.

When you're tuned in, which is to say in harmony with your surroundings—aligned with whatever is going on rather than at odds with it—you'll notice these connections and you can play with them, while delighting in the irony.

Welcome adversity as an unexpected gift,
Zen says.

Through all the interruptions, the provocations, and the unexpected incidents, keep your humor. What a tragedy it would be to have it swallowed up by feelings of indignation and resentment. These kinds of feelings coalesce into a poisonous mix, tainting what you project into the classroom and into the world. But every time you catch yourself spinning into those negative feelings, incensed by outrage and insult—*How dare he do that in my class!*—you curtail them. By catching them, you actively disallow them from growing, and you disallow yourself from getting hardened.

Of course, as teachers, part of our job is to keep order so that we can teach. But with a sprinkling of good timing and humor, we can make use of the unexpected and even the unacceptable. Zen emphasizes the comic rather than the detestable.

The corollary of a good sense of humor is that it is liberating, and no less so in the classroom. It dissipates tension and allows you to surmount any situation rather than being enslaved by it, or worse, victimized by it.

There is an old Zen story about a Chinese monk. Typically zany, like most Zen stories are, it recounts how Shui-lao became enlightened after his teacher kicked him in the chest. When his fellow monks asked him about it, he said, "Ever since the master kicked me in the chest, I have been unable to stop laughing."

Keeping our sense of humor intact is not only liberating, but it's also a way of saying *Yes* to all of life, even when what is delivered is as desirable as phone solicitation. Seeing the adverse as an opportunity is to embrace life rather than resist it, which is what it means to live an enlightened life. Rather than seeing enlightenment as some unattainable, mysterious phenomenon that happens only to the lucky ones in some faraway mythical land, look upon it as the spontaneous joy that swells forth with the acceptance of every moment, however fleeting, and with whatever that moment brings.

As a final thought on adversity, welcoming it is not the same as tolerating it, but we can reproach the conduct rather than the student. That in itself restores perspective and humor. When a toddler breaks his toys, we blame his lack of development, and when our elders forget important dates, we attribute it to their age. We forget that in between, we are all a work in progress and that we bear the same foibles that get us all into trouble at some time or another, even when no one else sees. We all fail to control ourselves. We sulk and rage, and forget to act our age. But when we remember to remember this, we nurture a different perspective and prepare ourselves to respond to unexpected provocations with more skill. As if unfurling from a chrysalis, the beautiful colors of poise and serenity begin to emerge, which in turn bring true, heartfelt patience—the sort that comes from understanding rather than from merely biting our tongues. There comes a point when we find we aren't as easily annoyed by others.

We will never be able to completely control our environment, not even our classrooms, but we can learn to see things differently. It is only through this wider perspective that we can take advantage of whatever pops up . . . even the weeds.

"there is some critical point where it gets so bad the absurdity of it all overwhelms you and you can do nothing but laugh. At that moment you up level your predicament, you see the cosmic joke in your own suffering."

—Ram Dass, *Journey of Awakening: A Meditator's Guidebook*

17

Names
Pay Attention, Would You?

I had 128 students in a single class one semester, and I had all but given up on learning their names. I read one name after the other on the three-page roster without looking up. *Make sure I can hear you so I don't mark you absent,* I would say. Sometimes I didn't bother taking role at all.

I was struck and a bit embarrassed when reading an interview by David Foster Wallace, the American writer who recently killed himself. He talked about his determination to memorize his students' names when he taught creative writing at the university: "It's going to take me, like, two weeks to learn everyone's name, but by the time I learn your name, I'm going to remember your name for the rest of my life."[6]

On the one hand, they're only names; everyone forgets names. But I realized that not even *trying* to learn my students' names was just an indication

---

6. D.T. Max, "The Unfinished." *The New Yorker*, March 9, 2009.

of something else going on. It wasn't really about names—it was about my waning interest.

But it is the low points in life that evoke awakenings.

One day there were students sitting in the doorway of my classroom. One of them looked familiar, and after class he came to my desk to say hello. I asked if I knew him and whether he had previously been in one of my other classes. He said that yes, he had been, but we knew each other, really, from The Deck—the restaurant by the beach—where he had served my husband and me many times.

I was embarrassed, and I sensed that my failure to even recognize him had hurt his feelings. I tried to excuse myself by asking if he had recently changed his hair. To my relief, he said he had. He had, in fact, just cut it short. "I knew something was different," I added, exaggerating the impact of the changed appearance.

He said his name was Nathan, and I said I'd be sure not to forget it next time.

Dharma: The Lesson for Teachers

Have you ever had the opportunity to observe the Japanese tea ceremony? In tranquil presence of mind, the host attends to the multifarious ritual with deliberate attention to every detail. Nothing is overlooked or disregarded as inconsequential. The tea ceremony is a meditation in motion whose every movement beckons our awareness so that mind and movement are one.

Japanese haiku poetry provides another opportunity to contemplate the respect given by the Japanese to the fine points, never glossed over for being plain and commonplace; it is, after all, the ordinary business of life, the everyday rituals, and the multitudinous sights and sounds that reveal the essence and spark of life. In this haiku, the poet hears the cuckoo's voice as if for the first time:[7]

> *Hidden among the roots of grass*
> *I hear a cuckoo.*
> —Otsuin 1807

Nourished on the same tenuous island lands, both traditions—the tea ceremony and haiku poetry—flicker with the sober light of Zen and its gentle nudge to not only stay present, but also to be *interested.* For in this fly-by-night, capricious thing called life, we have nothing to do but cherish the impermanence. A hundred years are but a flash in time.

Being interested means dropping the distinction between the spectacular and the mundane. It all *is.* It means coming back to the state of awareness found in the midst of the everyday chores we tend to rush through in order to get to the more interesting stuff. But in this state of rushing, our awareness is deadened, making it impossible to recognize and seize the charm in the repetitive chores that are an inevitable part of the everyday. How much time we spend on these things, and how much of our lives shall we then throw away for disregarding their importance and for neglecting the splendor of it all?

The classroom is the everyday. And yet, at the same time, every day it is new. But discovering its newness requires new eyes, born from the genuine spirit of interest.

---

7. Yoel Hoffman. *Japanese Death Poems.* North Clarendon, VT: Tuttle, 1986.

Knowing names just for the sake of it is merely symptomatic. Being *interested* in the names is just as good—it shows your interest in *them*, which matters more than whether or not, or how fast, you succeed in actually remembering their names.

Act as if, Zen says.

And if you're not truly curious? Ask questions anyway. Act as if you were.

When my own teacher suggests this deceptively simple method for turning bad habits around, it is sometimes met with suspicion. *Do you mean I should be fake?*

Acting *as if* is permission to do differently, to cultivate new behavior, and to establish new habits. We often assume that we *act* as we *feel*, but the opposite is true as well. Reconditioning our habits simultaneously reconditions our brains. It rewires the entire network that controls our behavior, carving out new neural tendencies and breaking us out of limits we have been placing on ourselves for years. Even our very core beliefs shift as a result, since to *live* a new reality is to directly *experience* a new reality. Direct experience shatters what we are used to believing about the world. We come to *know* differently by *doing* differently. And by *doing* differently, we can *be* differently so that finally then we can *see* differently.

Acting *as if* is about experience first—not beliefs. Thus, it is not about telling yourself something that you don't really believe. It is not about repeating affirmations. It's about doing. Acting *as if* is a way of conditioning different behaviors, of allowing yourself to experience the world in different boots so that it will then become the new way.

Try an experiment the next time you walk into class a few minutes early: Ask a quiet student what he did over the weekend and whether he enjoyed himself, and if not, why not. Ask him what his major is. Compliment someone, and mean it. These little moments are transformative. They emit a glimmer of light that is felt by all—you, the student, and everyone else around you. A spontaneous connection is made because it's *right*—it's what we're supposed to do as humans. There's an inexplicable "rightness" about entering into the present instead of drifting off into your head or squirreling yourself away under your lecture notes. And in those moments, a spontaneity takes over, leaving in its wake an all-around excitement to be *here*.

I often have fun with their names while taking role, and as long as I'm having fun, they're having fun. They're engaged, and we quickly bond as a class. Rhyme with the names if you're feeling zany, share an anecdote if you have a friend with the same name, or ask about the name's country of origin. Share something about your own name. The everyday chore of taking role becomes an opportunity to show interest, shape relationships, and brighten the mood. Thus, we discover a greater significance in the most ordinary of tasks—in this everyday chore, you open your heart not only to them, but to this moment, and to all of life.

18

The Coveted A
Desperate Demands

The inevitable barrage comes about a week after the close of every semester. That's the time it takes me to give final exams, read them, and calculate final grades. On their end, many students have been checking every hour, on the hour, at their computers, clicking the appropriate link until the coveted data shows up. As soon as I click SUBMIT on my end, it's sometimes only a matter of minutes before they see it. And then, like suitcases tumbling down the chute at the O'Hare baggage claim, the e-mailed grade-change requests come flooding in.

Theses requests come in many varieties. There are the presumptuous ones, the disgruntled ones, and some that play the victim; the desperate ones, the angry ones, and those that butter me up. Some are couched in elaborate excuses, while others are downright shameless. Often they are not requests at all—they are undisguised demands. Or unflinching negotiations. They haggle for the grade they want as if it were a leather jacket in the bargain district downtown. Whether subtle or explicit, they all cite their concerns over their grade point average (GPA), explaining that they can't possibly transfer into a four-year university with a B on their transcript, so they have to get the A, and since they got As in their other classes, they have to get an A in this class too, *so please let me know asap when we can talk about this.* Their myriad petitions often include a compliment about the class, as in this e-mail, which I've left unedited:

> *I took your Philosophy 22 class, I wouldn't know if you remember me, from fall semester. This is ————. I wanted to know if I can receive an A. I'm ready to participate in any sort of extra credit, or even go to places regarding attachment to the course. Im ready to do a research paper or even an essay on any subject you inquire. I really look at my transcript, and I need an A instead of a B. My gpa has dropped alot. I really appreciate the inlightenment you put in me, especially the courage in understanding the eastern world and dualism. I learned alot from you and the class. Again, thank you for your care and valuable time.*

They come tumbling down the chute faster than I can pick them up:

> *To be honest with you i was one of the students that if im not mistaken u marked points off for talking in the class, i dont know if you remember me. i am willing to do anything in order to get an A, as this really hurts my gpa.*

After verifying that there had been no mistake on my part, and after explaining the inappropriate nature of such a request—of asking to do extra assignments after the semester is over, assignments that the other students would never have access to—most surrender their appeal. But sometimes they persist, if only to let me know the extent to which I've personally sabotaged their college dreams, such as this one from a young man with a flair for the dramatic:

OK, fine. you're the boss, but i hope you always remember that because of the grade you gave me, i was unable to send my application to UCLA, and now my future is over, to say the least. so, merry xmas and happy new year!

The subject line of these e-mails usually reads MY GRADE. I open them up, read them, and reply by explaining anew, each time, the unacceptable nature of what it is they're asking for. And then one day I posted a universal note on my homepage, summarizing these responses, hoping it would deter some of the requests:

To all students who earned a B, but wanted an A:

- *Everyone wants an A. That doesn't mean instructors are obliged to issue them to everyone.*
- *Everyone is concerned about their GPA. Your GPA concerns are not relevant to the instructor's grading process.*
- *Your grade is based on merit, not on the instructor's desire to please each student, or worse, on the fear of disappointing the student.*
- *I can't speak for all instructors, but I won't compromise my ethics and risk repercussions by offering special, secretive assignments to individual students after the semester is closed. So, please don't ask! After all, everyone could bring up their grade if given the chance to do extra assignments!*
- *There are many others in the class who ended up with the same total points as you, and received B's; should I also give them A's? If so, where should I draw the line? The grade margin would then cease to mean anything, and grades would become nothing but a random whim.*
- *In my world, A's and B's are both good grades. And it's too bad SMC doesn't allow half grades, because that would allow me to assign a B+ or an A- where applicable.*

- *I'm sorry you're disappointed with your B, but it's your choice to be disappointed.*
- *Finally, if you truly liked and benefited from my class as you say you did, you would have learned the ideas of acceptance and humility.*

Sometimes the negotiations are preemptive. A student will come in person near the end of the term, asking to see the roll book, adding that she just wants to see how many absences she has. "But I was there!" she'll say, after assessing the check marks, or lack thereof, next to her name. "Why didn't you check in with me?" I'll ask. One day, a colleague who shares my office, self-described as "at her wits' end" with the mountain of grade-change requests, blurted out to one unsuspecting petitioner: "Now, at the eleventh hour, you're suddenly concerned?" Without meaning to, I smiled the smile that pops up involuntarily out of solidarity.

Dharma: The Lesson for Teachers

When there is no anger inside, there is no enemy outside.
—Lama Zopa Rinpoche

The dramatic e-mail I'd received—*now my future is over*—had to have come from an overwhelmed kid who was enmeshed in the confusion of transferring, and suffering from all that goes along with it—the deadlines, the forms, the finances. He was undoubtedly feeling swallowed up by an inflexible system that is inherently and inevitably competitive.

California leads the country in transfers from community colleges to four-year universities, and given pervasive problems like overcrowding and underfunding, the competition to get in is more severe than ever. Such problems have led to widespread campus protests led by students and teachers alike. One student told me he was denied entrance to UCLA with a 3.6 grade point average. Although there may be more to the story, keeping these things in mind—and remembering that the fierce pressure on students leads easily to distress and discouragement—helps us to keep our reactions to their demands in perspective. Look at the begging as just one visible component of a broken machine.

The student felt victimized by these circumstances and conditions, and having been told that his future depends on getting through the surplus of ever-increasing hoops, he doesn't see an alternative but to negotiate his jumps. Most university-bound students are in the same position, feeling just as desperate, and in their minds, they are at the mercy of the gatekeepers that will determine their futures. Understanding this will lessen the tendency to feel outraged by their demands, even when they seem unreasonable.

Of course, their desperation doesn't mean that anything goes, that anything is excusable. It doesn't mean my students' unreasonable demands are acceptable. And it doesn't mean I have to like the sense of entitlement that comes through in the tone of many of these e-mails. But better understanding tempers our own reactions.

In a subtler sense, each e-mail has intrinsic value just for being sent by a different individual. Its individuality makes each one, by definition, new. In the midst of our irritation with the requests as a whole, it's all too easy to forget this evident fact. Remembering is to stop seeing them as a *thing*. Remembering this snaps us out of the abstract *idea* of them and lets us see them instead as something real and fresh and personal each time.

Holding them at arm's length, seeing each one not as unique but as just another tedious grade request, tends to make us aloof. It also fosters the tendency to see them all—funny as it sounds—as *the enemy*, that annoying thing that pops into your inbox again just to spite you and irritate you. A fleet of irritants, each demanding a response. Contributing to the annoyance are our memories of having received countless others, similar in purpose, after each semester's end. We have to remember that none of the petitioners are focused on the fact that a thousand others have also asked.

I remember another evening at Guru Singh's yoga class. The kundalini master said to *keep going*. And we continued to push, up-and-down, up-and-down, up-and-down. Some of us slow, others faster. It didn't matter as long as it was with the breath and with unbroken focus and concentration, until movement and breathing became one event. *Don't give yourself exhaustion signals*, he urged. Lift-and-squat, lift-and-squat, lift-and-squat. But it wasn't about the squat. It was about getting past our usual patterns of opposition. *Dissolve the distinction between pushing against gravity and lifting with levity*, he continued.

Through the seemingly endless repetitions of the exercise, we were made to face our own resistance. The point was to discover our "edge" and the self-imposed blocks that come up every time until there is nothing left but to surrender. It's the place where we meet up with the complaint department, known as "the ego." It's where we take the opportunity to look at the conditioned behavior that we hold up with equal parts pride and resignation, proclaiming that it's "just who we are." In accepting the opportunity to look at these patterns rather than resist them, we also resist the inclination to jump away from the discomfort that goes along with looking. The idea is to come out stronger, more stable and more able, and less bound by the teeter-tottering of our own minds—all the longing and loathing, all the distinctions that support the ego's needs for identification, power, and control.

A good spiritual teacher knows that only there, in the fray, can we see our resistance for what it really is: ego-consciousness. The purpose is not to hurt ourselves trying to become enlightened, but to see that the mental quality of aversion is just conditioning, which gives rise to knee-jerk reactions that are a bit like those car alarms that seem to go off all the time for no reason at all.

Recognizing our own false alarms has the amazing effect of disarming them and dissolving the armor that keeps us hardened. In this case, the hardening shows in our resistance to those e-mails. *They're a waste of my time*, we might say. Just be aware when those reactions come up. Simply looking at them allows you to discover, in the process, the genuineness of each e-mail, as if it were the first one ever. And then the shift occurs. You start acting from the heart and from a desire to help rather than from a desire to punish the sender for sending the request. It doesn't mean we deal out As just because they asked, but we can respond with openness and sincerity. I used to wonder sometimes if I should cop a tougher attitude, but the mere consideration of such a question just keeps us in the realm of the abstract and precludes natural, heartfelt action. Those kinds of questions are nothing but head stuff.

When we allow ourselves to get swallowed up by the feeling of annoyance, it is at a heavy cost—our humanity. So it's a matter of recovering the humanity that is so easily forgotten when dealing with our day-to-day hassles. Ironically, it is often in the midst of those aggravations that we rediscover it, which is why the spiritual masters always say to be grateful to whatever and whoever provokes. Those are the situations that give us the opportunity to practice patience and compassion. They push us to confront our discomfort, so then even when the answer is *No*, it's a sincere *No*.

"As long as you don't realize that your real enemy is within you, you will never recognize that the mind of attachment is the root of all the problems your body and mind experience."

—Lama Yeshe, *Ego, Attachment and Liberation*

PART Three

·

PHILOSOPHIZING
BURNOUT

·

19

Passion
Accept, Adapt, and Abandon Hope

Y*ou should feel passionate about what you do!*
We've all heard this credo many times, proclaimed with the conviction of a scientific law. A mere mention, a simple suggestion, a reluctant insinuation of your burnout, and it will be broadcast with renewed persuasion: *Follow your passion!* or, *Have you lost your passion?*

The invitation to chase our vocational passion, with passion, guides us through many of life's important decisions, from what we major in to what city we live in. And in Hollywood, chasing our calling might even influence who we marry if the connection is likely to open the doors to the job of our dreams.

Crazy as that sounds, it does seem reasonable to assume that if we're enthusiastic about what we're doing, and well-suited for it besides, then we'll do a better job and serve the world more effectively. As some philosophers have suggested, we actually have a *duty* to do what we're suited to do for the sake of the community. But, I always wondered, what happens if we don't happen to (always) enjoy what we happen to be good at? Is that even possible? It would be a bit like asking, What if Barbra Streisand didn't enjoy singing? I can't imagine those songs I grew up with sung by any other voice. I can't speak for her, but it would be unreasonable to assume she loved to sing all the time. As with all careers, enthusiasm waxes and wanes, and not all aspects of the activity are equally enjoyable. Besides, like anyone else, she's probably good at many things. So, according to those old philosophers, which thing would she have a stronger duty to do? The flip side would be, What happens if we don't happen to be good at what we happen to enjoy? In other words, when our skills don't match our desires?

And the emphasis in our culture is always on personal desires. Perhaps that's why we pay such reverence to the term *passion*, which has become synonymous with any intense desire, despite its original meaning. Before the modern era, it described suffering—a kind of pathology as derived from the Greek word for sickness, *pathos*. The crossover in meaning is ironic, considering that from the Buddhist point of view, relentless desires are the very source of our suffering and chronic dissatisfaction in life. Thus, Buddha, like his fellow yogis before him, understood that in order to eradicate suffering, we had to let go of the incessant desires and attachments that keep us perpetually frustrated. The spiritual idea is to *stop being a slave to your passions*. Especially since the very nature of the word *passion* suggests an intensity that is the antithesis of balance and moderation.

What about people like Jane Goodall and Gandhi, who are rightfully applauded for having followed their passions? This is a mistaken way of looking upon their missions. These are the rare few who, conversely, put their own needs aside for the sake of the greater good. They were free of the egocentric mind and the personal desires it generates and acted on behalf of others. They lived to serve and were guided by a sense of justice and conviction rather than by personal desires. They were willing to renounce personal desires for a cause. Further, each acted with patience and discretion—in Gandhi's case, his willingness to regularly call off marches if things threatened to get violent demonstrated his total lack of any attachment to a time-based agenda.

In light of their selfless service and subjugation of personal needs, I would suggest that the term *passion,* in its modern sense (as synonymous with *desire*) fails to describe the scope of their actions. Both of these saints would be better described as committed and dedicated to their respective causes. And they were com*passionate,* in that their motivation stemmed from their capacity to *suffer with* the beings they fought so hard to save, and in Goodall's case, those she selflessly continues to save.

But I hadn't really considered it yet, and one day, in between classes, I sat near the newly constructed fountain and reflected on this question of vocational passion. As a tired instructor in an overcrowded classroom, in need of a break, I also wondered about my own waning enthusiasm. Had my passion died? If I'm supposed to be passionate, and I'm not, I reasoned, then I'd better do something else with my life before it's too late. After all, I've still got some good years left. And there it was again, that cultural refrain, like some popular song stuck in my head: *You should do what you love, and love what you do!*

But at the same time, I had a feeling there was something misleading about it, something quixotic; the insistence on undying fervor, the expectation of continued excitement, at the intensity of a teenage love affair and toward one destined career, expected to last until retirement, because that's your purpose in life. It seemed like an unrealistic expectation, hardly grounded in reality. The shiny surface of the golden baton we all counted on to lead the way was tarnishing.

My suspicion took the form of a series of observations and questions.

What about when someone is passionate about inappropriate things? Horrible examples abound. They should absolutely not be allowed to do what they love, especially if it is harmful to others, and less so if they are in a position of power, where they can do even more harm all around. But then, when there is no power at all, there is usually little choice, as shown by the many unfortunate people doing undesirable jobs, not only in developing parts of the world, but in advanced countries as well, particularly in the wake of a major recession where you take any work you can get. For countless millions, it would be mere indulgence to entertain the fantasy of finding their *true passion*. Totally unrealistic, starry-eyed hedonism of the modern world. So we might not want those with a lot of power chasing their passions, and there's often no way for those who have no power at all to even consider the pursuit.

I went back to Barbra. Even if she happens to love singing all the time, I mused, there are undoubtedly many people who are no longer excited by the work they're so good at. And the reverse is also true: It's the paradox of not being good at what you'd really love to do. I used to be that paradox. I remember staying home "sick" from school as a kid so that I could sing along with those very songs that could only be sung by Barbra. Then I'd croon all the mellow '70s pop, songs by Carly Simon and Carole King, and I'd shamelessly belt out the classic rock too, like Heart and Elton John. I knew the entire *Yellow Brick Road* LP, which I remember flipped open into three parts and even had the lyrics. The problem is, I can't sing! So, not only might it be the case that you don't *want* to do what you happen to be good at, but it can also go the other way—you may find out you're not particularly suited for what you really *do* want to do. And that can be a predicament if you're not willing to let go of the unrealistic dream. Oh, I still sing; I just do the world a favor and close the car windows at red lights.

The real problem with our fixation on passion is the near certainty that even a blazing fire will dim with time. Then what? Even when passion is pursued and found, the affair won't last forever. Passion changes. We change. A dancer friend recently shared with me the common experience among the cast members of a famous musical. Far from reveling in prideful accomplishment for having been part of one of the longest-running shows, they're sick and tired physically, and mentally jaded. Many are dancing on old injuries and are scarcely able to find the motivation to go onstage night after night; yet somehow they manage to put themselves into their postures and glissade, on tiptoe, onto the stage, one more time, because it's how they make their living. It is the same motivation that gets most of the world to work every day.

It reminds me of the ancient Greek myth about Sisyphus: He is condemned by the gods to push a gigantic boulder up a hill, over and over, all day long, even as it continuously rolls to the bottom of its own weight as soon as he gets it to the top. The gods understood the futility of wasted labor, so assigning it was the perfect, wicked punishment. In retelling the story, the French philosopher Albert Camus likens the absurdity of the task to the everyday predicament of every single one of us, pushing our rocks in our own way as we struggle to meet deadlines, deal with coworkers and bosses, and solve the problems that are part and parcel of any workday, anywhere.

But Camus was an optimist. Despite his fate, it is Sisyphus himself who decides to be happy. He can whistle and hum happy songs while he pushes his rock, or he can lament and endlessly curse his fate. The irony is that as soon as he realizes the power inherent in his own reaction, he is liberated. He makes his fate his own. It is he alone who decides to be happy or miserable. In a nod to our own capacity for liberation, Camus says, "We must imagine Sisyphus smiling."

Dharma: The Lesson for Teachers

Sisyphus's existentialist smile resonates with the Buddhist reminder to let go. Sisyphus smiles because he accepts his fate. To let go is to accept. And through acceptance, Sisyphus liberates himself from his sentence. To accept is to simultaneously stop resisting. When you stop resisting, you are able to enjoy your experiences, which is to say, your life.

> *Accept, adapt, and abandon hope,*
> Zen says.

During one of my teacher's dharma talks, he shared this message with us, telling us to *accept, adapt,* and *abandon hope.* In my mind, these three magical words took the form of an acronym, AAA. To the Western way of thinking, the idea of acceptance contradicts everything we've been nurtured to believe, especially our insistence on going after what we want and to never settle for less. Settling is seen as meekness in our culture.

> *Don't wear two heads,* Zen says.

But acceptance isn't meekness; rather, it is the wisdom to cease combat. It is the wisdom Sisyphus shows when he smiles even as his boulder falls unavoidably to the bottom of the hill one more time. It is a willingness to stop pushing our agenda on the world and the wisdom to know that pushing engenders frustration. It's about honesty. The time may not be right to make a change. Are you going to suffer every day until it is? The suffering is extra. And therefore, it is likened in Zen to the absurdity of wearing two heads. My Zen teacher would say, "You're fantasizing."

Some people find a dream vocation haphazardly, falling into something by way of an unexpected offer or other such happy accident. There's no point in being miserable until that time comes. And what if it never comes? I remember reading about filmmaker Kathryn Bigelow, director of the award-winning *The Hurt Locker*. She was already a talented painter when she found her way into filmmaking, and she described how one fortified the other. The same is true for many of us. Steve Martin was a stand-up comedian until *The Jerk*. After the success of his hilarious first film, he never had to earn a living as a stand-up comedian again. We see later how one aspect of our lives made possible something else that came along at a different time. It would be difficult and almost silly to try and pinpoint the one true passion when each had its time and place and purpose. We evolve. Passions evolve. The bigger point is that everything gets old and boring after a while. In the spirit of the song "Love the One You're With," can you be fine where you are before going elsewhere?

Only when we let go of our agendas can we be truly free, and only then can we *adapt* to any situation without slipping into the tendency to judge it according to our preferences or run from it. It is laying down the *picking and choosing mind,* but instead of succumbing to defeat like a soldier laying down his sword, we are at once liberated. No longer will we be looking for our fulfillment on the outside.

Finally, if the third part of the acronym, *abandoning hope*, seems upon first glance to be pessimistic, consider it from another perspective. It invokes the art of living in ease, of no longer being enslaved by all the grumbling, nor by the never-ending impulses— wishing for this and pining for that, and never being happy because nothing is ever *right*. As an everyday application of this teaching, think of those days when it seemed like you got stuck at every red light, having to brake just when you were gaining momentum: Give up! *Abandon hope!* And just when you do, when you slow down and enjoy the ride, the lights seem to open up and turn green for you, like magic.

When you've put the dragon to rest, a most welcome feeling of peace swells up in the space that was once occupied by resistance. When we are at peace, we can be good teachers. We can rediscover the joy that had gone missing, and our students will have more fun in the process. We have for so long associated that joy with the quality of passion—especially as teachers, where it is bound up with the altruistic aspects of our profession, of wanting to do good by our students. But to do good by anybody, we have to be *here* for them, which, obvious as it may sound, is the opposite of where most of us are at any given moment. We're normally stuck in our heads, wishing we were somewhere else, or even *someone* else. Only when we can come back to the vitality of true presence of mind and give our full and complete attention to the task at hand—without preconceived ideas of how things should be, and without resistance of any kind—can we be of any real service to anybody. And only without resistance can we really be *here*.

Being here starts by accepting whatever *here* brings, even the parts we're used to complaining about. All jobs include a certain element of drudgery; there is no job that is all glamour. But that's when we turn to our wisdom and we start to accept. Then we adapt and abandon hope, and we find the joy in whatever the activity is. The kind of people who love their jobs forever and who always seem to be happy are those who can find the beauty in almost anything, because they are open and present for their lives. They are like Sisyphus.

As teachers, we are entrusted with the near-sacred task of elevating young minds. Recognizing the value of this charge is in itself a great joy. After all, it's fun to help others, and it's even more fun when we're here, wholeheartedly, to do it.

20

Sartre and Buddha
True Freedom Is a Settled Mind

In my Philosophy of Film class, we had just watched *Waking Life,* the partially animated movie about philosophy, where actual characters—washed over in wavy watercolors—explore life's fundamental questions in the context of the main character's lucid dream. In one of the early scenes, a philosophy professor celebrates the empowering nature of Sartre's existentialist philosophy. Contrary to what people think, "Sartre never had a day of despair in his life," he explains to the curious dreamer.

Sartre's philosophy is described as empowering because of the way he approaches one of philosophy's biggest questions: *Does life have meaning?* He says we create meaning through the choices we make. We define our own purpose. But it requires tapping into our inherent freedom of choice. As we create our own identities through the decisions we make, we realize our potential as humans. We carve out our own paths. And for the iconic French existentialist, that's what *authenticity* is all about.

In philosophical terms, it means rejecting the traditional notion of destiny and the corresponding idea that things are inevitably the way they are, set and fixed, in a preplanned universe. There is nothing preplanned, according to Sartre, so he famously rejects such a thought. Thus, he rejects *determinism*, since it suggests a preexistent, predetermined plan. Sartre asks, Where is this plan? Since determinism leaves no room for free will, it opens up a world of convenient excuses that make it too easy for us to dodge responsibility for our actions, allowing us to fall back on such clichés as *That's just the way I was made*, and, *It was in the cards*, or, *It must have happened for a reason*.

For Sartre, these excuses won't do. We need to pull ourselves up and make the most of whatever our situation is, given the choices available. He is an unrelenting champion of free will, and it is that very unyielding commitment to internal freedom that makes him an existentialist. As conscious beings we are innately free, but that freedom comes with a price, namely the burden of responsibility. Only when we embrace this absolute responsibility for every decision we make, only when we *own* our existence, shaping it through the choices we make, do we live an *authentic* life.

Having already taken my Asian Philosophy class, one perceptive student raised his hand and asked whether Sartre's authenticity is comparable to the Buddhist teaching of *mindfulness*—the deliberate state of pure awareness that allows us to resist the deeply engrained patterns of negative mental conditioning by simply staying present. This student saw the kinship in the shared emphasis on internal freedom.

Insofar as Sartre encourages us to actively create our own fate, with all the responsibility that comes along with this freedom, there is a parallel, but Sartre's freedom has more to do with *conscious choosing* than one's *state of consciousness*. There is a difference. Put another way, Sartre's free will is said to be a product of our consciousness. But this typically unaccommodating consciousness is exactly the source of trouble from the Buddhist perspective! It is the ego-mind with its never-ending roster of grudges and complaints that is the source of all irritation.

In practice, the difference between Sartre's inner freedom and Buddha's inner freedom is immense. The first is an ability to freely choose from among alternatives that exist in the world, while the latter refers to an awakened state of mind that liberates us from ego-consciousness. An awakened state of mind shapes what we perceive as *choices* in the first place and shapes how we see the world and our place in it and, more importantly, engenders *acceptance* when the choice we want isn't available. In this enlightened state of mind, we come to *see* the world differently, and act differently in it. Actions are the inseparable corollary of our state of mind. This is what it means when Buddhist teachings say that *mind* shapes the world. Mind *is* world.

Philosophy, whether Eastern or Western, isn't supposed to be merely cerebral. Disregarding the old caricature of the armchair philosopher, it should apply to life; it should be something to turn to when times get rough.

While burnout may not rank high on the list of human maladies and afflictions, it can feel like a game of internal tug-of-war in which your own mind plays two roles: *I'm so burned out / You have it so easy / I sing the same song every semester / Be grateful you have work.* This kind of schizophrenic dialogue is typical of the ego-mind, the nothing-is-ever-right mind, and left to its own devices, it'll chatter on unchecked. Such is the power of habit. I wanted to be able to turn to the philosophy I had studied and taught for so many years in an attempt to find some answers.

I saw that from the point of view of the existentialists, like Sartre, I am the master of my life, my vocation, my relationships, my character, and everything else. So, I reasoned, if the spark has drained from the work I am doing, I could choose to simply walk away. After all, according to the existentialists, to continue on in quiet resentfulness is to live an *unauthentic* life. *Take control of your life*, Sartre would say. *Navigate your own ship!*

After class that day, still abuzz with *Waking Life* and my student's question about freedom, I considered my own blahs. The palpable feeling of internal resistance only intensified. Was I navigating my own ship? I convinced myself that I was playing a role, *playing professor*, since if I didn't want to do this work and I was doing it anyway, then I was merely putting on a show. The ironic consequence is that when I considered it this way, I ended up feeling very *in*authentic—the opposite of what I was supposed to feel, according to the French philosopher. Hardly liberated, I felt that it was inevitable I'd continue to get sucked into a cesspool of resistance and negativity as long as I continued spinning. Like those annoying radio commercials, the inner chitchat chattered on—no matter how many essays on free will I read.

Here's why: When these thoughts come up, we are distracted by what we *should* be doing rather than present for what we *are* doing. The *should* is additional and conditional. I *would be*, and I *could be*, if only some other condition was met first. It is like saying, *I will be happy only if, and only when* . . . And whatever is additional, the Zen masters say, is as absurd as having two heads.

As to the question of the meaning of life, the Zen masters of old might simply point to the clouds. *What is the meaning of their beautiful glide across the autumn sky? What is the meaning of the exquisite sound of Vivaldi's* Four Seasons?

Dharma: The Lesson for Teachers

All the "existential angst" Sartre speaks of—a mouthful of a term, referring to the burden of our responsibility as free and forlorn creatures in a non-determined universe—slides all too easily into more of the same spinning thoughts that fill our busy heads and our entire existence. And that's not to shun responsibility; it's to shun the tiresome ruminations.

> *It's the work of the ruminating mind,*
> Zen says.

We're attached to these thoughts because they provide the illusion of control. By repeating scenarios in our heads, we convince ourselves that we're managing things. Opening to the truth of how little in life we actually *do* get to control reveals the busy headwork as a futile waste of energy and vitality, yet for some reason, we continue to cling to these thoughts out of habit. Strangely, it becomes part of our identity, so, just like remaining in an unhealthy relationship, we repeat this behavior because it's familiar.

Letting go of what Zen refers to as the *ruminating mind* is truly liberating. How do you let it go? By simply letting it go. How do you drop anything? The ruminating mind will offer its barrage of wearisome, repetitive thoughts, and then they will go away, so long as you don't attend to them and feed into them. You just come back *here*. It's a practice: You keep coming back to being present, and eventually, the thoughts will dissipate on their own. Like unwanted solicitors, they get tired of knocking on your door after a while.

When the water is clear, you'll know
what to do, Zen says.

Tending toward analytical thinking, I wondered what my Zen teacher meant when he assured me I'd still know what to do if I summoned up the courage to let go of my neurotic thoughts. *Knowing* in the Zen sense does not involve concepts or ideas, as it does in the West; it is a quality of uncluttered presence that inspires grace in action.

And this state of presence—what my student meant by *mindfulness*—brings us into direct contact with *what is* so that we can get along in the world, even when it's not as we planned or according to our expectations. Next time you find yourself indulging in the false panacea of negativity, out of habit, take a chance and come back to presence. It's so uncomplicated, but because habits can be relentless, it takes practice. Just keep coming back.

The habit of negative thinking is made stronger by stress and boredom; both push us into what feels familiar in a hopeless attempt to find shelter. The familiarity comes at too high a price, however, since for many of us, it's the ruminating, spinning mind that serves as our go-to routine. Coming out of it doesn't have to be complicated. Simply recognize that negative aspect of your mind. Recognize the chatter for what it is—just chatter. A kind of magic happens with the simple act of staying present without getting caught up in the stories we all concoct inside our heads and without reacting to the drama going on up there. The *real* show is going on here and now. So with compassion for yourself, just keep coming back.

Liberation means freedom from old habit patterns. It is all the mental whirling that keeps us everywhere but here and that prevents clarity and joy. When we're not here, we're not living our lives. Notice that on those occasions when you forget to do something, or you do something you didn't really want to do, it's on account of not being present. Your mind was elsewhere. The paradox is that there is nowhere else to go but here. When we pull ourselves up out of this eddy of thoughts, we find that suddenly, the world takes on a new radiance.

Acknowledgments

When this book was but a notion, a pale and distant glimmer at the farthest reaches of my mind's eye, it was author and Zen priest Karen Maezen Miller who was ready with wise encouragement and spot-on suggestions. I am grateful for her guidance and friendship.

It is a blessing when new friends appear at just the right time, especially in the rugged early stages of an author's first book, when any signpost in this unknown terrain is a boon. Author Darren Littlejohn provided such direction at a time when I had none. To him I owe a debt of gratitude.

To my dear teacher and mentor, author Dr. Larry Payne, who happily read over some ungroomed chapters when this book was still in the making and lovingly offered his support, I now offer my sincerest thanks. I am humbled by the trust he so readily placed in me to carry on our treasured yoga lineage.

One day my future agent, Kate Epstein, paused upon some sample chapters about a burned-out college instructor and her classroom chronicles and found within them something of value and benefit. I'm so glad she did, and so thankful to have her guidance. The home she would eventually find for this project would be with a publisher who shared her enthusiasm for its content and who would see to it that its stories would be shared. To Skyhorse, and especially to my dear editor, Ann, for having championed my work early on and for her invaluable suggestions and insights, I offer my warmest thanks.

Without my spiritual practice and those who have compassionately guided it, this work would not exist. For this support, I am indebted to my teachers, both in Zen and in the yogic traditions, especially Guru Singh, whose teachings have long been a source of inspiration, and my beloved Zen master, Nyogen Yeo Roshi—I hope I can someday fulfill his hopes for me.

I am grateful to my dearest friend and colleague Elissa Kyriacou, whose stories and conversation were instrumental in the early development of this work.

Lastly, my appreciation goes out to my students, for the lessons I've learned from them, and especially to my son and husband, for their undying love and encouragement.